french

Sue Purcell

UNIVERSITY OF
CAMBRIDGE

Published by BBC Worldwide Ltd.
Woodlands, 80 Wood Lane, London W12 0TT

Developed by BBC Languages

Development manager: Debbie Marshall

Project editor: Josie Frame

Project assistant: Melanie Kramers

Design: Pentacor

Layout: Jo Sproat

Illustrations: Sophie Joyce and Anna Wray

Production controller: Man Fai Lau

Cover design: First City Advertising

Cover photographs: (tl), (tc), (tr), (cl), (c), (bl) Corbis;

(cr), (bc) Getty Images; (br) Robert Harding

Picture research: Sally Spray and First City Advertising

Cambridge Team (The Language Centre, University of Cambridge):

Executive Director: Anny King

Head of IT: Christoph Zähner

Project Manager: Anita Ogier

Project Secretary: Penny Godfrey

Printed and bound in Great Britain by ESP Colour Ltd, Swindon

Get Into French includes:
– 2 x PC CD-ROM
– 60-minute audio CD
– 144-page book
– online activities and resources
  at www.getinto.com/french

contents

COURSE MAP   4
FIND WHAT YOU'VE LEARNT ON THE CD-ROM

HOW TO USE THE COURSE   6

INTRODUCTION: LEARNING A LANGUAGE   10

1 FIRST CONTACT   16

2 EATING AND DRINKING   27

3 ACCOMMODATION   38

4 GETTING AROUND   48

5 ASKING THE WAY   58

6 SIGHTSEEING AND LEISURE   68

7 BUYING FOOD   75

8 SHOPPING   83

9 CHATTING AND SOCIALISING   94

10 PAST ACTIONS, FUTURE PLANS   101

GRAMMAR   113

ANSWERS   138

		first contact	eating and drinking	accommodation	getting around	asking the way	sightseeing and leisure	buying food	shopping	chatting and socialising	past actions, future plans
CD–ROM **book unit**		**1**	**2**	**3**	**4**	**5**	**6**	**7**	**8**	**9**	**10**
AT THE HOTEL											
1. Booking a room				●							
2. Checking in				●	●						
3. Making a complaint				●							
4. Checking out				●	●						
IN THE BAR											
1. Ordering drinks			●								
2. Talking about what you do and where you're from		●									
3. Chatting about what you like doing		●								●	●
4. Making arrangements										●	●
5. Chatting about what you did at the weekend											●
IN THE RESTAURANT											
1. Having a snack			●								
2. Ordering a meal			●								
3. Asking for extras and appreciating the food			●								
4. Settling up			●								
AT THE CAMPSITE/BEACH											
1. Checking in				●			●				
2. Finding out about activities							●				
3. Finding out about local attractions						●	●				

	first contact	eating and drinking	accommodation	getting around	asking the way	sightseeing and leisure	buying food	shopping	chatting and socialising	past actions, future plans
	1	**2**	**3**	**4**	**5**	**6**	**7**	**8**	**9**	**10**

IN THE MARKET SQUARE

	1	2	3	4	5	6	7	8	9	10
1. Buying fruit and vegetables							●			
2. Shopping for meat and cheese							●			
3. Buying bread and cakes							●			
4. Getting advice from the chemist								●		

AT THE PETROL STATION/GARAGE

	1	2	3	4	5	6	7	8	9	10
1. Buying petrol and checking tyres				●						
2. Dealing with a breakdown				●						
3. Asking for directions					●					
4. Taking a taxi				●						●

IN THE DEPARTMENT STORE

	1	2	3	4	5	6	7	8	9	10
1. Asking where things are				●				●		
2. Buying gifts				●				●		
3. Shopping for clothes								●		
4. Buying shoes								●		
5. Meeting an old friend	●									

AT THE RAILWAY STATION

	1	2	3	4	5	6	7	8	9	10
1. Buying a train ticket				●						
2. Getting information at the tourist office						●				
3. Asking for directions in the metro				●						
4. Reporting a stolen bag				●						●

Welcome to **Get Into French**, the exciting new interactive course for beginners from BBC Worldwide and Cambridge University Language Centre. Ideal for people on the go, **Get Into French** has been designed to make your learning as efficient and as speedy as possible, while ensuring that the whole process is enjoyable and rewarding as well.

The four carefully co-ordinated elements of the course – CD-ROM, book, audio CD and website – create a total learning package, whose combined impact is far more powerful than the sum of its individual parts. The course brings several senses into play; you will see French written down, hear it on the CDs, speak it out loud and click on your mouse to engage in an active way. By encouraging your interaction from the outset, the course aims to get you communicating in French with confidence, fast.

THE CD-ROM

The CD-ROM is the core of the course. The eight language units, which comprise animated dialogues, interactive activities and instantly accessible learning support, give you the opportunity to listen, speak, read and write, promoting a good all-round understanding. The book, audio CD and dedicated website are all designed to supplement the CD-ROM.

decide how you learn

People learn in different ways and have different needs, and the design of the CD-ROM caters for this. Once you've created your on-screen persona, you can choose from a variety of locations in a fully animated virtual town, from restaurant to railway station, hotel to campsite. Each location provides the chance to learn and practise the key language needed in that particular situation; for example, in the bar you can learn how to order cocktails as well as chat to your fellow drinkers. These distinct topic-based units give you the freedom to decide exactly what is most relevant to your requirements. There are three main learning areas:

➤ You can choose to follow a structured learning path in the **Learn it First** area. Based on an animated dialogue that clearly presents the key language, engaging activities help you manipulate and extend the new words and phrases you encounter.

➢ When feeling more confident, you may then choose to tackle the **Have a Go** section, where you take part in a virtual conversation, recording your answers and comparing them with the voice of a native speaker.

➢ At any point you can set yourself a **Challenge**, where you take the part of a character in a particular storyline. This requires you to apply the French you have learnt so far, and an incorrect choice at any point will prompt you to return to the areas in which you need more practice.

learning support

In addition to the practical activities and tasks, there is an extensive built-in learning support area, which is available to you at all times.

Use the searchable **Phrase Book** to look up French words, or type in the English equivalent of what you would like to say. You can access whole phrases as well as individual words.

Essential information, such as times, dates and numbers, is presented in the **Basics** section. You can call this up at any time as a reference guide, or try out the activities for a more in-depth look at these areas.

Concise **Grammar Notes** pop up as you meet new language in the **Learn it First** dialogues. These allow you to learn the grammar in context, in short easy-to-grasp batches. If you decide you want a fuller explanation, you can just follow the link to the main body of grammar within the **Phrase Book.**

more than a language

Get Into French gives you an insight into France and how people live. Its intuitive navigation system means that you encounter information about French society in the relevant setting, at the same time as you learn the related language.

➢ When listening to a conversation in the **Learn it First** section, click on a **Cultural Note** icon and discover an interesting piece of information about the French way of life. Alternatively, you can access these through the **Phrase Book** search facility.

➢ Each animated location contains four special graphics that you can zoom in on for a closer look. Wander around the virtual hotel lobby, picking up the newspaper to check out the crossword, or read a film review in a local cinema timetable. These **Reading Activities** replicate material you will typically come across on a trip to France, and are an excellent means of extending your reading and comprehension skills.

ACCELERATE YOUR LEARNING

The book, audio CD and website all cover the core language of the CD-ROM, then add to it and develop it in different ways.

the book

Use this handy ten-unit book to revise and refresh the language you have met on the CD-ROM. The course map on pages 4 and 5 shows you at a glance which topics from the CD-ROM are covered in each unit, making it quick and simple to find what you're looking for.

Throughout the book you'll have the opportunity to read authentic French in a range of activities. Dip into the book wherever you are – take it with you when you go away or use it to prepare specific topics before you go.

the audio CD

This is designed to be used independently of the CD-ROM and book. It offers you another way of improving your understanding of spoken French, simply by listening to an interesting story. In a sequence of French and English conversations, you'll follow Simon Martin, a young British web designer, as he travels to Nice in search of new business.

You can choose to listen to Simon's story all the way through, seeing how much you understand, or you might prefer to take it more slowly, focusing on one unit at a time. If you feel you need extra support, you can refer to the scripts written in the accompanying booklet. Listen to it anywhere – in your car, on the move or at home.

the website – www.getinto.com/french

This dedicated site contains games and activities, extensive reading practice plus opportunities to learn about French culture around the globe. Just click on 'new user', and enter the following password:

FR31 P96T E2J8 GC7J

The **Get Into French** book is arranged by topic, rather than by location as on the CD-ROM. This is because, as you'll soon discover, many of the phrases you'll have learnt on the CD-ROM can be adapted to a wide variety of situations. For instance, 'asking for something' uses the same basic language structure whether you're in a bar or a restaurant, while the phrases for 'asking where something is' are the same whether you're inside a department store or asking for directions in your car. All you need to do is learn them once, and you'll be prepared for anything!

Your first port of call should be the course map on pages 4-5. This sets out the CD-ROM locations and the book topics in an easy-to-read grid, showing you at a glance where in the book to find out more about the language you've met on the CD-ROM. Alternatively, you can start at the beginning of the book and work your way through it from start to finish – either way, you'll be consolidating and extending your knowledge of French.

In each unit, you'll find lists of key phrases from the CD-ROM. If at any time you'd like to hear them in context, look for the 🌐 symbol, which refers you back to the appropriate section from the CD-ROM. You'll see that some of these key phrases are partly printed in bold type. These provide the basic 'toolkit' that will allow you to construct new sentences. Simply take the parts printed in bold type and add on vocabulary relevant to your situation.

Beneath the key phrases there are explanations of the most important language points covered in each set of phrases. More in-depth grammatical explanations are provided where indicated, and can be found in the grammar notes at the back of the book.

As well as key phrases and language explanations, you'll also find useful lists of vocabulary in each unit. Use these to build up your knowledge of French even further. You can then have a go at the realistic activities that feature throughout each unit. These are based on authentic material and are designed to extend your cultural knowledge and build your reading skills. You'll find the answers in the back of the book. These are intended as a self-check – do make sure you have a good stab at the activities before you look at them.

learning a language

Learning a language, like learning anything worth while, demands effort and commitment. Take no notice of claims by some language courses that you will be speaking fluently in a week, or learning effortlessly while you sleep; these are marketing gimmicks.

That said, there are several steps you can take to speed up your learning and avoid wasting time on unproductive activities, enabling you to make the most of **Get Into French:**

▶ Set yourself goals...

...both long- and short-term, but make sure they are realistic. Your long-term goal could be the time you specify for completing the course – you might allocate two weeks per unit. You can then break down your goals into weekly and daily targets, which might be to spend an average of an hour per day on learning and reviewing, or to learn ten new words every day. Tick off each goal as you reach it; you'll be amazed at how quickly you'll acquire a list of things you've achieved.

▶ Little and often...

...should be your watchword. Speaking another language is a skill, just like playing a musical instrument. As with music practice, it's better to spend 20 minutes twice a day on your French than to have a marathon three-hour session on a Sunday evening. If you use 'dead time' to revise – when you're on public transport, sitting in the car waiting for the kids to come out of school, waiting for the kettle to boil – the time spent on studying won't interfere with the rest of your life at all.

▶ Don't try to do too much...

...in one session. Pick a distinct, limited topic and concentrate on that. Rather than deciding to revise verbs in general, choose to look at just one tense formation, or pick two or three irregular verbs to learn thoroughly. Rather than having a vague idea of 'learning vocabulary', look at all the words you have come across that are related to buying a snack, say, or to hobbies.

▶ Save the things you find most difficult...

...or new material, until a time when you are feeling fresh and can study undisturbed. If you are feeling more tired, if something else, like driving, requires your attention, or if you are surrounded by noise and activity, spend your time revising material that you covered a week or more ago. The more you go over material that you have already covered, the more likely it is to pass from your short-term to your long-term memory.

▶ Don't be discouraged...

...if you appear to be making slow progress. It is the nature of language learning that the goalposts are constantly moving. You start off by thinking that you'd be very happy if you could order a drink in French. When you can do that, you realise that what you'd really like is to understand the barman's response. Then you think how nice it would be if you could have a brief conversation, and so on. Your aspirations and expectations increase, and there's always something new that you don't know. Think in terms of how much you already know, and what you *can* say.

▶ Get together with a friend...

...or family member who wants to learn French too. That way you can compare learning experiences, help each other and practise conversing in French. Just knowing that you've made an agreement to do certain things before you next meet can maintain your motivation and enthusiasm.

▶ Don't be afraid of making mistakes...

...Mistakes are a natural and vital part of the learning experience. Treat your study sessions as rehearsals, times when you can be adventurous and try out things you've just learnt – or even things you haven't quite learnt. Talking of rehearsals, really act the part when practising your French. Speak out loud – even if the dog and the plants are your only audience! Record yourself on tape, and listen critically to your performance. Before you reach for a dictionary, have a guess – more often than not you'll be right, and guessing prepares you for dealing with ordinary conversations in France, when you won't be able to keep looking things up.

▸ Learn vocabulary in context...

...rather than as a list of unrelated words. It's much easier that way. Rather than just learning ten words a day at random, choose a topic – food items, clothing, colours. Putting words in a sentence helps you to remember better too. If your topic for the day is fruit and vegetables, put the words into sentences beginning **je voudrais, donnez-moi** or **vous avez?** After all, this is how you are most likely to use these words in real life.

▸ You don't need to know how to say everything...

...There are some things you will probably never say in French, you will usually only hear them – like prices or directions. Don't waste time trying to put 'take the second on the right' or 'it costs 13 euros an hour' into French. Check you understand by looking at or listening to the French only. When you're reading French, chances are you won't need to know every word; it's more likely that you will need to scan a piece of writing to pick up key points or to get the gist. This is something we do all the time in our native language and is a valuable skill to master in French.

▸ Learn set phrases...

...such as **Vous pouvez répéter, s'il vous plaît?** *Can you repeat that please?* **Vous pouvez parler plus lentement?** *Can you speak more slowly?* **Je n'ai pas compris le mot...** *I didn't understand the word...* You won't then be stumped when you meet with a fast-speaking French person or with a new word.

▸ It's difficult to unlearn bad habits...

...so get used to checking things – gender and verb endings, for instance – right from the start. When you learn nouns, learn their gender with them, so rather than saying **pomme, citron, fraise**, say **la pomme, le citron, la fraise**. It takes no longer, but it helps you reach the stage where you will know what sounds right and what doesn't.

▶ Recognise patterns in French...

...All languages are based on rules and patterns, even if there are exceptions. If you recognise **-ez** or **-ir** as verb endings, it will help you to guess what they might mean in English. Realising that a word ending in **-ment** in French **(vraiment, seulement, exactement)** is often the equivalent of a word ending *-ly* in English *(really, only, exactly)* makes learning vocabulary and comprehension easier.

Above all, enjoy learning French with **Get Into French!**

Bonne chance! *Good luck!*

major differences

There are many similarities between French and English, which means that you'll often be able to guess at the meaning of French with some certainty. **Le restaurant est au centre de Paris** is very like *The restaurant is in the centre of Paris*. But there are also some striking differences in the way the two languages work.

word order

Possibly the most immediately obvious difference is word order in certain circumstances: *French wine* is **vin français**; *Where are you from?* is **Vous venez d'où?** (you come from where?).

gender

In French, inanimate objects as well as people are either masculine or feminine, and this has knock-on effects. There are masculine and feminine versions of *a*: **un homme** but **une femme**; and *the*: **le vin** but **la bière**. Also, the words you use to describe something (adjectives) change their ending to match what they're linked to: **le vin blanc** but **la carte blanche**, **un bon restaurant** but **une bonne salade.** A man says he is **sportif**, whereas a woman is **sportive**. Sometimes the difference cannot be heard, although it is written differently: a man says **Enchanté** for *Pleased to meet you*, and a woman says **Enchantée**, although both sound the same.

levels of formality

In English you use *you* whether you're talking to one person or several people, close friends or complete strangers. In French there are two different words for *you*.

- **Tu** is used when you are talking to one person you are on very close terms with. It's used with friends, family and when talking to children.

- **Vous** is used when talking to one person you don't know well, or when in a more formal situation. It's the most useful word for *you* when on holiday in France and is the word you will use to address shop assistants, hotel staff, waiters, etc. **Vous** is also used when talking to more than one person, even if individually you would address them as **tu.**

◨◧◨ verb endings

In English, you put words like *I*, *you* or *they* in front of a verb to indicate who you're talking about. The verb itself changes very little: *I prepare, you prepare, he prepares.* French also has words for *we*, *you*, etc, but the ending of the verb changes for each of them. *I prepare* is **je prépare**, *we prepare* is **nous préparons** and *you prepare* is **vous préparez**.

If you look up *prepare* in the dictionary, you'll find the basic form **préparer** – known as the infinitive. There are many other verbs ending in **-er** that have the same set of endings. There are two other main verb groups (ending in **-ir** and **-re**) with similar, but slightly different, sets of endings.

Besides these three groups, French has many irregular verbs, which have to be learnt individually. Some of the verbs you will use most often are irregular: **être** *to be*, **faire** *to do* and **vouloir** *to want*.

◨◧◨ forming questions

Questions are formed differently in the two languages. Compare the English statement *You work* and the question *Do you work?*. French is much more straightforward. The wording of statements and questions is often the same: **Vous travaillez** *You work*, **Vous travaillez?** *Do you work?* It's the tone of voice that makes it clear that the latter is a question.

An alternative way of asking questions is to put **est-ce que** at the beginning of the statement: **Vous travaillez** *You work*, **Est-ce que vous travaillez?** *Do you work?*

◨◧◨ other differences

The differences highlighted here aren't the only ones that exist between English and French. You'll come across many others, for example:

- *The* has a plural in French: **le citron** but **les citrons,** and **la tomate** but **les tomates**.
- Some notions, such as age, are expressed differently. In French you don't say *I'm 27*, but **j'ai 27 ans** (*I have 27 years*).

The important thing is to look out for and work with the differences, rather than trying to translate English into French word for word.

first contact

hellos and goodbyes

- saying hello
- introducing yourself and others
- saying goodbye

chatting about yourself

- saying where you're from
- saying where you live
- saying what you do

chatting about your family

- describing your personal situation
- talking about your family

infrarouge

hellos and goodbyes

▢▢▢ saying hello

> **Department Store 5;**
> **Basics, First Contact, Greetings**

Salut!	Hello, hi!
Bonjour.	Good morning, hello.
Bonsoir.	Good evening.
Ça va?	How are you? (informal)
Comment allez-vous?	How are you? (formal)
Ça va.	I'm OK.
Ça va bien, merci.	I'm fine, thanks.
Ça fait plaisir de te revoir.	It's nice to see you again.

There are two words for *you* in French: **tu** and **vous**. **Tu** is informal and tends to be reserved for chatting with friends and younger people in general – people you might say a casual *Hi* to in English and **Salut** in French. **Bonjour** and **bonsoir** can be used to greet anyone, including people you don't know, such as staff in hotels, shops and restaurants, and people you know on a formal footing. It's usual to address such people as **vous**, until invited to use **tu**, and it's polite to add **monsieur** or **madame** after **bonjour**. **Vous** is the one you should use if in any doubt at all. (Remember, **vous** is also used when talking to more than one person.)

Ça va? is an informal way of asking how someone is. You need to make sure it sounds like a question (with your voice rising on **va**) when using it in this way, because the same two words **ça va** can also be your answer to **Ça va?** You can add to this: **Ça va bien** *I'm fine* or **Ça va très bien** *I'm very well*. **Va** and **allez**, in the more formal **Comment allez-vous?**, both come from **aller**, which literally means *to go* and which you'll come across in all sorts of other circumstances. *(You can find more on **aller** in the grammar section on page 126.)*

 ## introducing yourself and others

 Basics, About Me, Name

Comment vous appelez-vous?	*What is your name? (formal)*
Comment tu t'appelles?	*What is your name? (informal)*
Je m'appelle Christine, et toi?	*My name is Christine, and you?*
Moi, **je m'appelle** Marc.	*I'm Marc/My name is Marc.*

Je m'appelle literally means *I call myself*. Putting **moi** before it adds emphasis to the **je**, which is done in English simply by pronouncing the word *I* with more emphasis. The verb in French that means *to be called* – **s'appeler** – is a reflexive verb.

Basics, First Contact, Greetings

Je te présente ma femme, Marlène, et mon fils Pierre.	*Let me introduce my wife Marlène and my son Pierre. (informal)*
Je vous présente mes parents.	*May I introduce my parents. (formal)*
Voici David, un ami.	*This is my friend David.*
Enchanté(e).	*Pleased to meet you.*

Mon, **ma** and **mes** all mean *my*. The choice depends on what follows, not on the gender of the speaker. Regardless of who is speaking, *my father* is **mon père**, *my mother* is **ma mère** and *my children* are **mes enfants**. (*You can find more on* **mon**, **ma**, **mes** *– possessive adjectives – in the grammar section on page 117.*)

Enchanté(e) *I'm pleased to meet you* describes the speaker, so you'll see an extra **e** written when a woman is speaking. It makes no difference to the pronunciation.

In the sentences **Je vous présente…** and **Je te présente…**, **vous** and **te** literally mean *to you (I present to you)* and they go in front of the verb, just like the **vous** in **s'il vous plaît**, which literally means *if it pleases you*. (*You can find more on object pronouns in the grammar section on page 118.*)

saying goodbye

**Department Store 5; Bar 3;
Basics, First Contact, Greetings**

Au revoir.	*Goodbye.*
À bientôt.	*See you soon.*
À ce soir.	*See you this evening.*
À plus tard.	*See you later.*
À vendredi.	*See you on Friday.*
À très bientôt au bout du fil.	*Speak to you soon on the phone.*

À means *at*, *to* or *until*, and is often used with a time to indicate when you'll next see each other. It can precede virtually anything – in this context days of the week, dates and times of day. **À** cannot be followed by **le** – they combine to make **au**, which explains **au revoir**: **à + le revoir**, literally *until we see each other again*. *(You can find more on* **à** *in the grammar section on page 122.)*

🟨🟧🟥 saying where you're from

> **Bar 2; Basics, About Me, Nationality**

Vous venez d'où?/Tu viens d'où?	*Where do you come from? (formal/informal)*
Vous êtes d'où?/Tu es d'où?	*Where are you from?*
Je suis sénégalais(e).	*I'm Senegalese.*
Je suis du Canada.	*I'm from Canada.*
Je viens de Dakar.	*I come from Dakar.*
Je suis originaire de Belgique et français(e) de nationalité.	*I'm originally from Belgium and I have French nationality.*

When using **venir de** and **être de**, you need to keep the article (**le** and **les**) with countries that are masculine singular and masculine plural. For example, **Je suis du** (de + le) **Canada**, **Je viens des** (de + les) **États-Unis** *I come from the United States.* For feminine countries just use **de**, as in **Je viens de France** *I come from France,* **Je viens d'Angleterre** *I come from England.* With towns, always use **de: Je viens de Dublin.**

> **key vocabulary – countries and nationalities**

l'Angleterre (f)	anglais(e)	*England/English*
l'Irlande (f)	irlandais(e)	*Ireland/Irish*
l'Écosse (f)	écossais(e)	*Scotland/Scottish*
le pays de Galles	gallois(e)	*Wales/Welsh*
la Grande-Bretagne	britannique	*Britain/British*
la France	français(e)	*France/French*
l'Allemagne (f)	allemand(e)	*Germany/German*
l'Italie (f)	italien(ne)	*Italy/Italian*
le Canada	canadien(ne)	*Canada/Canadian*
les États-Unis	américain(e)	*American*

Nationalities in French are not written with an initial capital letter: **je suis sénégalais.** Feminine forms usually add an **-e** or, in some cases, **-ne.** Remember that this added **-e** means you sound the final consonant. If the masculine form ends in an **-e**, the feminine doesn't change.

saying where you live

Bar 2; Basics, About Me, Residence

Vous habitez où?	*Where do you live? (formal)*
Tu habites où?	*Where do you live? (informal)*
J'habite à Paris, **en** France.	*I live in Paris, in France.*
Je suis de Grenoble.	*I'm from Grenoble.*
Je suis à Paris **depuis** cinq ans.	*I've been in Paris for five years.*

To say *in* + a town, you use **à**, for example **à Paris** *in Paris*. However, with a country, you use **en** if it's feminine: **en France** *in France*, **en Angleterre** *in England*, **en Afrique** *in Africa,* or **au** if it's masculine: **au Canada** *in Canada*, **au pays de Galles** *in Wales*. A few countries are plural, and with these you use **aux:** eg **aux États-Unis** *in the United States*, **aux Pays-Bas** *in the Netherlands.*

Depuis is used when conveying the English *have been (doing something) for (a period of time).* The accompanying verb in French is in the present tense, because the action is still going on, **J'habite au Canada depuis deux ans** *I've been living in Canada for two years. (You can find more on* **depuis** *in the grammar section on page 132.)*

saying what you do

Bar 2; Basics, About Me, Profession

Qu'est-ce que tu fais?	*What do you do?(informal)*
Qu'est-ce que vous faites (comme travail)**?**	*What (sort of work) do you do? (formal)*
Quelle est votre/ta profession?	*What is your profession? (formal/informal)*
Je travaille à Nanterre.	*I work in Nanterre.*
Je suis programmeur/ programmeuse.	*I'm a computer programmer.*
Je suis enseignant(e).	*I'm a teacher.*
Je travaille dans un bar.	*I work in a bar.*
Je travaille pour une banque internationale.	*I work for an international bank.*

Most adjectives in French come after the noun, unlike in English: **une banque internationale.** They agree with the noun they describe; **internationale** is feminine to agree with <u>une</u> banque (**international** is the masculine form). *(You can find more on adjectives in the grammar section on page 115.)*

(You can find more on adjectives in the grammar section on page 115.)

---

key vocabulary – occupations

masculine	feminine	
infirmier	infirmière	*nurse*
étudiant	étudiante	*student*
mécanicien	mécanicienne	*mechanic*
avocat	avocate	*lawyer*
employé	employée	*clerk, worker*
coiffeur	coiffeuse	*hairdresser*
programmeur	programmeuse	*computer programmer*
serveur	serveuse	*waiter/waitress*
professeur	professeur	*schoolteacher*
comptable	comptable	*accountant*
médecin	médecin	*doctor*
architecte	architecte	*architect*
réceptionniste	réceptionniste	*receptionist*
dentiste	dentiste	*dentist*
secrétaire	secrétaire	*secretary*

Many professions have different masculine and feminine versions. The ending **-eur** has the feminine form **-euse**, **-ier** becomes **-ière** and the masculine **-ant** adds an **e** in the feminine. Other common patterns include **-ien** in the masculine form, which becomes **-ienne** in the feminine, and jobs ending in **-é** in the masculine, which end **-ée** in the feminine. Others use the same word for both men and women.

When talking about your profession in French, leave out the word for *a* or *an*, simply saying **je suis dentiste**, for example.

have a go

1 soap box

These are parts of some dialogues from a French soap set in Créteil, just outside Paris. Two new characters, Julien and Rachid, are being brought into the series.

▶ From these scripts, what could you say about the two newcomers?

Mimi: Julien, je te présente ma mère. Maman, je te présente mon fiancé, Julien.

Maman: Comment? Ton fiancé? Mais... alors... enchantée, Julien.

Julien: Bonjour, madame. Enchanté.

Maman: Vous venez d'où, Julien?

Julien: Je viens du Sénégal, mais j'habite à Meaux depuis cinq ans.

Didier: Salut Jean-Pierre! Ça va?

Jean-Pierre: Oui, ça va bien. Et toi?

Didier: Super bien. Jean-Pierre, je te présente mon collègue Rachid.

Jean-Pierre: Bonjour, Rachid. Tu travailles aussi pour la banque d'affaires?

Rachid: Oui, je travaille avec Didier. Je suis analyste programmeur.

▶ You've seen how the soap stars do it. A brief introduction is something you often need to give about yourself. Would you be able to do one? Practise it out loud.

mais	*but*
moi aussi	*me too*
la banque d'affaires	*merchant bank*
avec	*with*
un analyste programmeur	*programmer-analyst*

❯ chatting about your family

◻◻◻ describing your personal situation

 Basics, About Me, Marital Status

Vous êtes marié(e)?	*Are you married? (formal)*
Tu es marié(e)?	*Are you married? (informal)*
Je suis célibataire.	*I'm single.*
Je suis divorcé(e)/séparé(e).	*I'm divorced/separated.*
J'habite avec ma compagne/mon compagnon.	*I live with my partner.*

Marié, **divorcé**, **séparé** and **fiancé**, ending in **-é**, refer to men. Women need to add an extra **-e** although this doesn't affect the pronunciation. **Célibataire**, like other adjectives ending in **-e** in the masculine form, is used for both men and women.

◻◻◻ talking about your family

 Basics, About Me, Family

Tu as des frères et des sœurs?	*Do you have any brothers and sisters? (informal)*
Vous avez combien de frères et sœurs?	*How many brothers and sisters do you have? (formal)*
J'ai un frère et une sœur.	*I've got one brother and one sister.*
Je n'ai pas de frères et sœurs. Je suis enfant unique.	*I haven't got any brothers or sisters. I'm an only child.*
J'ai une petite sœur de douze ans.	*I've got a younger sister of 12.*
Vous avez quel âge?	*How old are you? (formal)*
Tu as quel âge?	*How old are you? (informal)*
J'ai trente ans.	*I'm 30.*

Notice how the word for *some* or *any*, **des**, becomes **de** after a negative verb in French. So it's **Vous avez <u>des</u> frères?** *Have you got any brothers?*, but **Je n'ai pas <u>de</u> frères** *I haven't got any brothers.*

Similarly, after **Combien....?** *How many.....?*, you need to use **de** not **des**:
Vous avez combien <u>de</u> freres? *How many brothers do you have?*

(For more on using negatives, turn to page 43, and to the grammar section on page 135. For more on using **de** *to mean 'some' or 'any', turn to page 121 of the grammar section.)*

J'ai trente ans – French uses the verb **avoir** *to have* when talking about age (literally *I have thirty years*). **Tu as quel âge?** literally means *What age do you have?*

(For more on using negatives, turn to page 43, and to the grammar section on page 135. For more on using de to mean 'some' or 'any', turn to page 121 of the grammar section.)

key vocabulary – family

le mari	*husband*	la femme	*wife*
le père	*father*	la mère	*mother*
le frère	*brother*	la sœur	*sister*
le fils	*son*	la fille	*daughter*
le grand-père	*grandfather*	la grand-mère	*grandmother*
le petit-fils	*grandson*	la petite-fille	*granddaughter*
l'oncle	*uncle*	la tante	*aunt*
le neveu	*nephew*	la nièce	*niece*
le cousin	*cousin*	la cousine	*cousin*

have a go

2 chit chat

You and your friend are both learning French and come across a French internet chat site with the usual mix of messages.

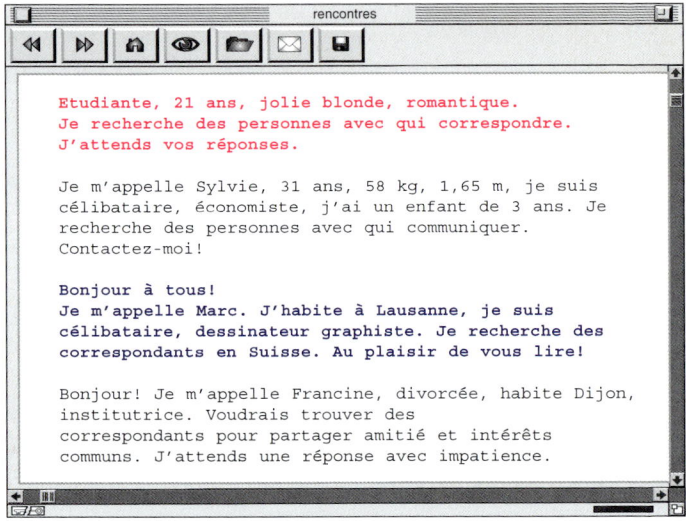

```
                                    rencontres

   Etudiante, 21 ans, jolie blonde, romantique.
   Je recherche des personnes avec qui correspondre.
   J'attends vos réponses.

   Je m'appelle Sylvie, 31 ans, 58 kg, 1,65 m, je suis
   célibataire, économiste, j'ai un enfant de 3 ans. Je
   recherche des personnes avec qui communiquer.
   Contactez-moi!

   Bonjour à tous!
   Je m'appelle Marc. J'habite à Lausanne, je suis
   célibataire, dessinateur graphiste. Je recherche des
   correspondants en Suisse. Au plaisir de vous lire!

   Bonjour! Je m'appelle Francine, divorcée, habite Dijon,
   institutrice. Voudrais trouver des
   correspondants pour partager amitié et intérêts
   communs. J'attends une réponse avec impatience.
```

▶ Your friend decides to post her own message. Could you help her by pointing out where in the messages she could discover how to say hello to everyone, and that she's a student, 22 years old, single, an attractive blonde, looking for people to chat to in France and she's looking forward to a reply.

la Suisse	*Switzerland*
je recherche	*I'm looking for*
Au plaisir de vous lire!	*Looking forward to reading your message!*
l'institutrice (f)	*primary school teacher*
partager	*to share*
j'attends avec impatience	*I'm looking forward to*
le dessinateur graphiste	*graphic designer*

UNIT 2

eating and drinking

ordering food and drink
- saying what you want
- finding out what's on offer

settling up
- appreciating the food
- asking for and querying the bill

❯ ordering food and drink

▢▢▢ saying what you want

 Bar 1; Restaurant 1, 2, 3

– Vous désirez?	– What would you like?
Un jus d'orange, s'il vous plaît.	An orange juice, please.
Je voudrais un sandwich au jambon, s'il vous plaît.	I'd like a ham sandwich, please.
Moi, je prends le plat du jour.	I'll have the dish of the day.
Pour moi, en entrée, les moules marinières.	For me, as a starter, the moules marinières.
– Vous prenez un dessert?	– Would you like any dessert?
Oui, **je prends** une glace à la vanille.	Yes, I'll have a vanilla ice-cream.
Je peux avoir la carte des vins?	Can I have the wine list?
Je pourrais avoir une carafe d'eau, s'il vous plaît?	Could I have a jug of water, please?

The simplest way of asking for something you know is available is to name it and add **s'il vous plaît**:

Le menu, s'il vous plaît *The menu please.*

To ask for something from the menu, you can use **je voudrais...**, **je prends...** or **pour moi** – and the waiter will probably respond with **Bien sûr** *Of course*, **D'accord** *OK* or **Merci** *Thank you*.

The question **Je peux avoir...?** followed by the item you want is a slightly more tentative request; use this form to translate the English *Can I have...?* or when you want to order something that you're not sure is available:

Je peux avoir une salade végétarienne? *Can I have a vegetarian salad?* You'll probably be told **Bien sûr** or **Sans problème** *No problem.*

Je pourrais avoir...? from the same verb, **pouvoir**, is an even more polite way of making the request:

Je pourrais avoir un steak-frites? *Could I have steak and chips?*

key vocabulary – snacks

un sandwich	a sandwich
au fromage	with cheese
au jambon	with ham
au saucisson	with sausage
au pâté	with pâté
une glace	an ice-cream
au chocolat	chocolate-flavoured
à la fraise	strawberry-flavoured
à la vanille	vanilla-flavoured
à la noix de coco	coconut-flavoured
à l'abricot	apricot-flavoured

Flavours and fillings: When talking about flavours and fillings, you use **à** + the + flavour/filling. However, **à** cannot be followed by **le** or **les**, so you use **au** before masculine singular nouns and **aux** with all plurals.

une glace <u>au</u> chocolat	a chocolate ice-cream
un sandwich <u>au</u> fromage	a cheese sandwich
un gratin <u>aux</u> courgettes	a courgette gratin
une glace <u>à la</u> fraise	a strawberry ice-cream
une soupe <u>à l'</u>oignon	an onion soup

The use of **à** indicates flavour or filling, not that the dish is made exclusively from this item. For example, compare the two items below.

une glace <u>à l'</u>orange	an orange-flavoured ice-cream (there are other ingredients)
un jus <u>d'</u>orange	an orange juice (made exclusively from oranges)

have a go

1 feeling peckish

You and two friends have stopped at a snack bar for a bite to eat and a drink. You're a vegetarian, Isobel fancies a ham sandwich and Meera is on a low-carb diet and refuses to eat bread, potatoes or pasta. You want a hot drink but you are avoiding caffeine. Isobel wants an alcoholic drink. Meera wants a non-fizzy soft drink but doesn't like fruit juice.

▶ What do you each order to eat and drink? (It turns out that you all order something different.)

MENU

Omelette nature
Croque-monsieur
Sandwich au jambon
Sandwich au saucisson
Sandwich au fromage

Boissons chaudes
Café
Cappuccino
Chocolat chaud

Boissons fraîches
Bière
Coca / Coca light
Jus d'orange
Eau minérale

 finding out what's on offer

Bar 1; Restaurant 1, 2, 3

Vous avez des salades?
Do you have any salads?

Qu'est-ce que vous avez comme sandwichs?
What sandwiches do you have?

– Nous avons des sandwichs au fromage et au jambon.
– We have cheese sandwiches and ham sandwiches.

Qu'est-ce que vous avez comme glaces?
What ice-creams do you have?

– On a des glaces au chocolat et à la vanille.
– We have chocolate and vanilla ice-cream.

– Je n'ai plus de glace à l'abricot.
– I haven't got any more apricot ice-cream.

C'est quoi le poulet basquaise?
What is chicken Basquaise?

Quel est le plat du jour?
What is the dish of the day?

Est-ce qu'il y a de la viande dans le gratin?
Is there any meat in the gratin?

Asking questions: Just as most English question words begin with *wh-*, the French equivalents begin with **qu-**.

qui?	*who?*
quoi?	*what?*
qu'est-ce que?	*what?*
quel?	*which? what?*
quand?	*when?*

There are exceptions: **pourquoi?** *why?*, **où?** *where?*, **comment?** *how?* and **combien?** *how much?* or *how many?*

(You can find more on asking questions in the grammar section on page 136.)

le pain	*bread*
le beurre	*butter*
le sel	*salt*
le poivre	*pepper*
le couteau	*knife*
la fourchette	*fork*
la cuillère	*spoon*
les plats	***courses***
le plat principal	*main course*
l'entrée (f)	*first course*
le hors-d'œuvre	*starter*
le dessert	*dessert*
les viandes	***meats***
la dinde	*turkey*
le poulet	*chicken*
l'agneau (m)	*lamb*
le bœuf	*beef*
le porc	*pork*
le canard	*duck*
les poissons	***fish***
les anchois	*anchovies*
le cabillaud	*cod*
la lotte	*monkfish*
le loup	*sea bass*
le saumon	*salmon*
le thon	*tuna*
la truite	*trout*
les fruits de mer	***seafood***
les crevettes (f)	*shrimp/prawns*
les moules (f)	*mussels*
le calmar	*squid*

have a go

culinary quiz

How well do you know French cuisine? Flicking through a French magazine you come across a quiz entitled *Testez votre connaissance de la cuisine française*.

▶ You have to match the descriptions to the name of the dish. Have a go. There is a clue to help you identify each one.

Testez votre connaissance de la cuisine française!

Ratatouille

Pour vous aider :
idéal pour les végétariens!

Salade niçoise

Pour vous aider :
il fait chaud et vous voulez un repas léger? C'est idéal!

Cassoulet

Pour vous aider :
vous avez très faim et vous adorez la viande? C'est pour vous!

A. C'est un plat traditionnel du sud-ouest à base de haricots et de viande de porc ou de saucisse de Toulouse, et de graisse d'oie ou de canard. L'ensemble est mis dans une cocotte puis au four pendant plusieurs heures.

B. C'est un ragoût de poivrons, courgettes, aubergines, tomates et oignons préparés à l'huile d'olive, qui peut se manger froid ou chaud en hors-d'œuvre, ou en plat principal.

C. C'est un plat qui comporte des haricots verts, de la laitue, des poivrons verts, des olives noires, des tomates, des filets d'anchois et des œufs durs. La salade se prépare sans vinaigre, en salant trois fois les tomates et en les arrosant d'huile d'olive.

▶ How many different vegetables can you find mentioned? What are they in English?

vous avez faim	*you are hungry*
avoir faim	*to be hungry*
le four	*oven*
manger	*to eat*

❯ settling up

🟨🟧🟥 appreciating the food

 Restaurant 3

– Ça a été?	– How was it?
C'était délicieux.	It was delicious.
Le poulet **était** vraiment excellent.	The chicken was really excellent.
La sauce **était** délicieuse.	The sauce was delicious.

The word **délicieuse** in the sentence **La sauce était délicieuse** is the feminine form of the adjective **délicieux** to agree with **la sauce**. If you wanted to say that the sauce, rather than the chicken, was excellent, you'd use the feminine form of excellent: **La sauce était excellente**. The 'default gender' is masculine; in other words, if a noun is not specified, use the masculine form of the adjective: **C'était délicieux** *It was delicious,* **C'était excellent** *It was excellent.* (*You can find more on adjectives in the grammar section on page 115.*)

Était, meaning *was*, is an example of the imperfect tense, which is one way of talking about the past. This tense is used here for a description in the past, rather than something you did or something that happened. (*You can find more on the imperfect tense in the grammar section on page 132.*)

key vocabulary – drinks

une carafe d'eau	*a jug of water*
une tasse de thé	*a cup of tea*
un café-crème	*coffee with milk*
le vin rouge	*red wine*
le vin blanc	*white wine*
une boisson (fraîche)	*a (cold) drink*
une bière	*a beer*
une bière blonde	*a lager*
un panaché	*a shandy*
l'eau minérale (f)	*mineral water*
une limonade	*a lemonade*

have a go

3 rave reviews

▶ You've just had a meal at the Bistro Saint Luc, a restaurant you chose mainly on the strength of the good reviews below.

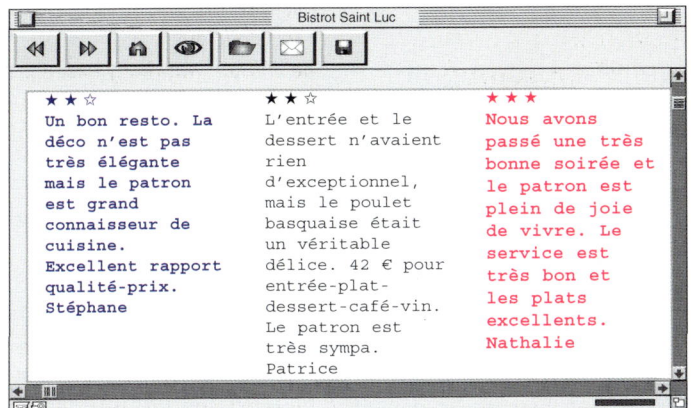

★ ★ ☆
Un bon resto. La
déco n'est pas
très élégante
mais le patron
est grand
connaisseur de
cuisine.
Excellent rapport
qualité-prix.
Stéphane

★ ★ ☆
L'entrée et le
dessert n'avaient
rien
d'exceptionnel,
mais le poulet
basquaise était
un véritable
délice. 42 € pour
entrée-plat-
dessert-café-vin.
Le patron est
très sympa.
Patrice

★ ★ ★
Nous avons
passé une très
bonne soirée et
le patron est
plein de joie
de vivre. Le
service est
très bon et
les plats
excellents.
Nathalie

▶ You thought it was a good restaurant, the food was excellent, the service very good and the owner was very nice. You decide to contribute to the forum by sending an e-mail to the site – you can use phrases from the reviews you have read.

🖋 Nul!   ☆ ☆ ☆ Bof...   ★ ☆ ☆ Bien   ★ ★ ☆ Très Bien   ★ ★ ★ Excellent

la déco   *decor (slang)*
le resto   *restaurant (slang)*

▨▨▨ asking for and querying the bill

 Restaurant 4

L'addition, s'il vous plaît.	*Can we have the bill, please?*
Le service est compris?	*Is service included?*
Excusez-moi, **je crois qu**'il y a une erreur.	*Sorry, excuse me, I think there's a mistake.*
Nous avons pris deux menus à 15 euros.	*We had two € 15 menus.*
Ce n'est pas grave.	*It's all right. No harm done.*

Nous avons pris literally translates as *We have taken* and is an example of the perfect tense, used to talk about something that has already happened. In French the perfect tense has two parts, equivalent in structure to English. This example combines **avons** (from **avoir** *to have*) and **pris** (a form of **prendre** *to take,* called the past participle; *taken* is the English equivalent).

To say *I* or *you* did something, you simply use the appropriate part of **avoir** with **pris** (which doesn't change). For example, *I had a sandwich* is **J'ai pris un sandwich**; *Did you have a sandwich?* is **Vous avez pris un sandwich?**

(You can find more on the past in Unit 10, and in the grammar section on page 129.)

have a go

4 **final reckoning**

You've had a pleasant meal but now it's time for the bill. You and your partner had one avocado salad, one onion soup, one grilled trout and one entrecôte, plus a jug of red wine. For dessert, you had raspberry tart and a fruit salad.

▶ Is the bill correct? Is service included?

Aux Ecrevisses
rue du Général de Gaulle
59000 Lille

Table: 8

1 Pichet Vin Rouge	
1 Salade d'avocat	8.50
1 Soupe à l'oignon	4.50
1 Entrecôte	5.00
1 Truite grillée	12.00
1 Flan aux abricots	10.50
1 Tarte aux framboises	3.50
	4.00
Total euro	48.00

Prix Net, Service 15% Compris
Merci de votre visite - à bientôt!

UNIT 3

accommodation

finding somewhere to stay
- making a booking
- checking in

while you're there
- finding out about facilities
- complaining about something

checking out
- paying and leaving

finding somewhere to stay

making a booking

 Hotel 1

Je voudrais une chambre **pour** deux personnes.

I'd like a double room.

Avec salle de bain/douche.
– Pour combien de nuits?
Pour deux nuits.
C'est combien?
Le petit déjeuner est compris?
– Le petit déjeuner est en supplément.
D'accord, **je la prends.**

With bathroom/shower.
– For how many nights?
For two nights.
How much is it?
Is breakfast included?
– Breakfast is extra.

OK, I'll take it.(the room)

checking in

 Hotel 2; Campsite 1

J'ai réservé une chambre.
Nous avons réservé un emplacement pour une tente.
Pour une semaine.
– C'est à quel nom?
Au nom de Jones.

I have booked a room.
We have reserved a pitch for a tent.
For one week.
– What name is it booked under?
In the name of Jones.

J'ai réservé and **nous avons réservé** are the equivalent of *I (have) booked* and *we (have) booked*. They are examples of the perfect tense. They illustrate how straightforward it can be to talk about what has happened. You use the present tense of **avoir** *to have* – **j'ai, nous avons, vous avez**, etc – with the past participle of a verb. **Réservé** is the past participle of **réserver**; other regular verbs ending in **-er** follow the same pattern: **téléphoner – téléphoné; dîner – dîné. Vous avez réservé une ou deux chambres?** *Did you book one or two rooms? (Talking about the past is covered more fully in Unit 10, and you can find more on the perfect tense in the grammar section on page 129.)*

have a go

1 mountain adventure

You plan to go on a week's holiday in the French Pyrenees with your sister and her two daughters aged 5 and 7, and you have found on the internet the details of a hotel called Hôtel Le Dauphin, near the Spanish border. You've drafted an e-mail to make the booking for the last week of October. This is the draft that you have sent for your sister to check:

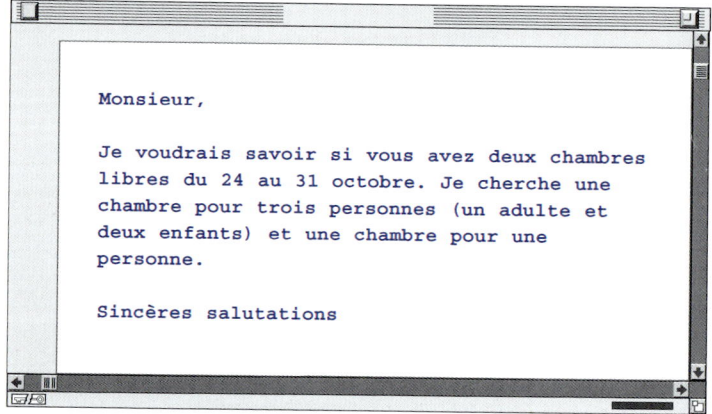

Monsieur,

Je voudrais savoir si vous avez deux chambres libres du 24 au 31 octobre. Je cherche une chambre pour trois personnes (un adulte et deux enfants) et une chambre pour une personne.

Sincères salutations

It turns out that there are two changes. Your sister now has to go a week later (2-9 November) and she also wants to take her other daughter, who is 15 and will want a room of her own.

▶ Could you write a new e-mail adapting the first one to include the necessary changes? Use a highlighter pen first to identify which words you will need to change – there are only six of them.

| je voudrais savoir si | *I'd like to know if* |
| sincères salutations | *kind regards* |

(For more help on simple letter and e-mail writing, have a look at the 'Basics' section of the CD-ROM.)

while you're there

finding out about facilities

 Hotel 1, 2; Campsite 1

Le petit déjeuner **est à quelle heure?**

What time is breakfast?

– De sept heures à dix heures.

– From 7am to 10am.

Est-ce qu'on peut dîner à l'hôtel?

Can we have dinner in the hotel?

Est-ce qu'il y a un restaurant?

Is there a restaurant?

– Nous avons un restaurant au premier étage.

– There is a restaurant on the first floor.

Qu'est-ce qu'il y a comme équipements?

What is there in the way of facilities?

– Il y a une petite épicerie.

– There is a little grocery shop.

Vous pouvez me recommander un restaurant?

Can you recommend a restaurant?

Est-ce que is a very useful little phrase that transforms a statement into a question without affecting the word order. **Vous avez une chambre** *You have a room*, **Est-ce que vous avez une chambre?** *Do you have a room?* **Il y a un bar** *There's a bar,* **Est-ce qu'il y a un bar?** *Is there a bar?*

Qu'est-ce que? meaning *What?* is equally useful and straightforward to use. **On peut faire** *One can do*, **Qu'est-ce qu'on peut faire?** *What can one do?*

(You can find more on asking questions in the grammar section on page 136.)

key vocabulary – hotel	
pension complète	full board
demi-pension	half board
un grand lit	double bed
un lit pour une personne	single bed
avec balcon	with a balcony
avec vue sur mer	with a sea view

have a go

speed dial

Below is a list of services offered by the Hôtel Métropole.

▶ What number would you dial if you wanted:

    a. a hairdresser?   b. to hire a car?   c. a beauty treatment?

    d. to get an outside line? e. to order a taxi?

L'Hôtel Métropole à votre service!

Réception		0
Baby-sitting	payant, cartes de credit acceptées,	
	consultez Réception	
		150
Blanchisserie		
Climatiseur	à contrôle individuel	
		225
Coiffeur		125
Concierge		
Excursions	voir Réception	
Fax	voir Réception	
Location		
de voitures	voir Concierge	
Restaurants	Restaurant Panoramique, 22e étage	170
	Restaurant Océane, specialisé en fruits de mer	195
		240
Room service		220
Salon de beauté		245
Sauna		
Taxis	voir Concierge	
Téléphone	directe; pour une ligne extérieure, composez le 9	
Thé et café	Un plateau courtoisie vous permettant	
	de faire du thé ou du café est à votre	
	disposition dans la chambre	
Voltage	220v	

There are various refreshment options available.

▶ What might you do if you wanted to:

    f.   have a cup of tea?

    g. book a seafood dinner for two?

    h. have breakfast in bed?

    i.   check if there's a table free for lunch in the top-floor restaurant, which has views over the city?

◻◼◼ complaining about something

Le téléphone **ne marche pas**.
Il n'y a pas de télécommande.
Le store **est cassé.**
– Quel est le numéro de votre
chambre?

The telephone is not working.
There is no remote control.
The blind is broken.
– *What is your room number?*

To make a verb negative in French, you put **ne** and **pas** around it:

Le téléphone marche.	*The telephone is working.*
Le téléphone <u>ne</u> marche <u>pas</u>.	*The telephone is not working.*

Je parle français.	*I speak French.*
Je <u>ne</u> parle <u>pas</u> français.	*I don't speak French.*

The negative of **il y a** is always **il n'y a pas** + **de**, regardless of whether you're talking about something masculine, feminine, singular or plural.

Il y a un presse-pantalon.	*There's a trouser press.*
Il <u>n'</u>y a <u>pas</u> de presse-pantalon.	*There's no trouser press.*
Il y a une douche.	*There's a shower.*
Il <u>n'</u>y a <u>pas</u> de douche.	*There's no shower.*
Il y a de l'eau chaude.	*There's hot water.*
Il <u>n'</u>y a <u>pas</u> d'eau chaude.	*There's no hot water.*
Il y a des chambres.	*There are rooms.*
Il <u>n'</u>y a <u>pas</u> de chambres.	*There are no rooms.*

This 'de after negative' rule applies after other verbs too:

Nous avons des chambres.	*We have got rooms.*
Nous <u>n'</u>avons <u>pas</u> de chambres.	*We haven't got any rooms.*

With **le store est cassé** *the blind is broken*, **cassé** is masculine because it describes **le store**. If a feminine item is broken, then you need the feminine form, **cassée**. For example, **la télévision est cassée, la radio est cassée**. This extra **-e** does not change the pronunciation. *(You can find more on adjective endings in the grammar section on page 115.)*

have a go

Disaster! You've arrived in your room, only to find the air conditioning isn't working, there's no soap and the coffee machine is broken. You don't know what number to ring for reception, and don't fancy queuing at the desk on your way out in the morning, so you decide to leave a note for the chambermaid.

▶ Fill in the gaps with the correct word chosen from the list below.

le savon	la télécommande	le store
la machine à café	le climatiseur	le téléphone

Madame,

Le .... ne marche pas. La .... est cassée et il n'y a pas de ....

Merci de votre assistance.

L'Hôtel Métropole

key vocabulary – hotel room

le presse-pantalon	*trouser press*
la machine à café	*coffee machine*
la télécommande	*TV remote control*
le climatiseur	*air-conditioning unit*
le store	*window blind*
le téléphone	*telephone*
le coffre-fort	*safe-box*
la fenêtre	*window*
la serviette	*towel*
le savon	*soap*
le shampooing	*shampoo*
le gel douche	*shower gel*
l'oreiller (m)	*pillow*
la couverture	*blanket*
le fer à repasser	*iron*
la prise de courant	*electrical socket*

key vocabulary – campsite

le bureau d'accueil	*reception*
l'eau chaude (f)	*hot water*
l'eau froide (f)	*cold water*
l'eau potable (f)	*drinking water*
le branchement électrique	*electrical connection*
le bloc sanitaire	*shower block*
la salle de jeux	*games room*
louer un VTT (vélo tout terrain)	*to hire a mountain bike*
la poubelle	*dustbin*
la pile	*battery*
l'ouvre-boîte (m)	*tin opener*
les allumettes (f)	*matches*

checking out

 paying and leaving

Hotel 4

Je peux avoir la note, s'il vous plaît?	*Could I have my bill, please?*
Vous êtes sûr(e)?	*Are you sure?*
Je crois qu'il y a une erreur.	*I think there's a mistake.*
Vous acceptez la carte Visa?	*Do you take Visa?*
Est-ce que vous pouvez m'appeler un taxi?	*Could you call me a taxi, please?*

Pouvoir *can, to be able* is usually followed by another verb. This second verb is always in the infinitive, while **pouvoir** changes depending on who is speaking:

Je peux/Nous pouvons avoir la note?	*Can I/we have the bill?*
Je peux/Nous pouvons réserver un emplacement?	*Can I/we reserve a pitch?*
Vous ne pouvez pas dîner à l'hôtel ce soir.	*You can't dine at the hotel this evening.*

Two other useful verbs, used in a similar way, are **vouloir** *to want* and **devoir** *must, to have to*:

Vous devez aller au commissariat.	*You must go to the police station.*
Je veux sortir lundi soir.	*I want to go out on Friday night.*

*(You can find more on **pouvoir**, **vouloir** and **devoir** in the grammar section on page 128.)*

have a go

4 happy families

You're planning a trip to the Auvergne region of France, and have found a website dedicated to holidaying in that region. You're thinking of giving the usual hotels a miss this holiday, as you'd prefer more contact with French people, life and culture. Ideally you'd like to stay with a French family who would provide meals. The website gives details of different types of accommodation available.

▸ Which ones will you investigate further?

▸ See how many words you can find in this advert that have very close equivalents in English.

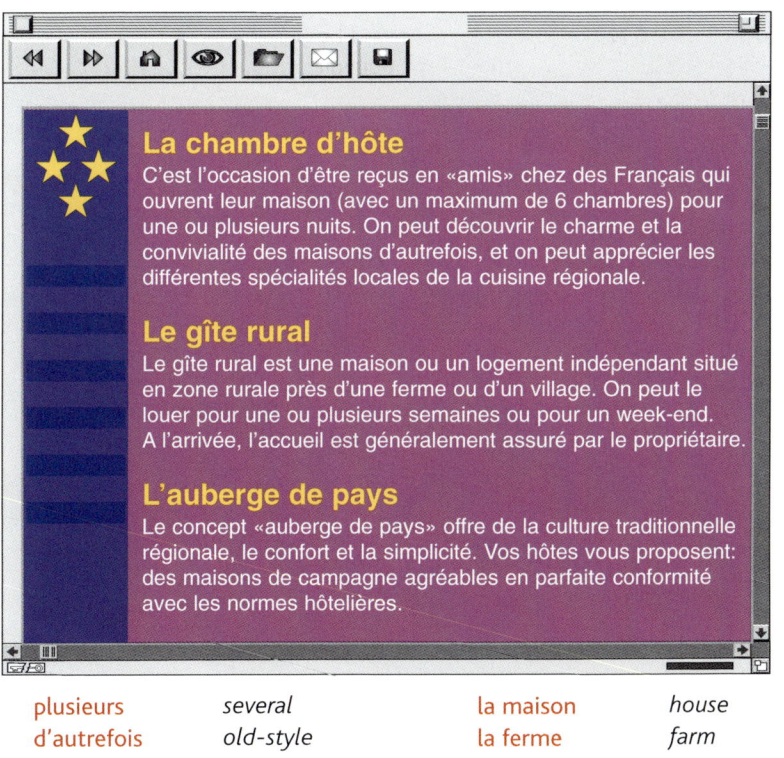

La chambre d'hôte

C'est l'occasion d'être reçus en «amis» chez des Français qui ouvrent leur maison (avec un maximum de 6 chambres) pour une ou plusieurs nuits. On peut découvrir le charme et la convivialité des maisons d'autrefois, et on peut apprécier les différentes spécialités locales de la cuisine régionale.

Le gîte rural

Le gîte rural est une maison ou un logement indépendant situé en zone rurale près d'une ferme ou d'un village. On peut le louer pour une ou plusieurs semaines ou pour un week-end. A l'arrivée, l'accueil est généralement assuré par le propriétaire.

L'auberge de pays

Le concept «auberge de pays» offre de la culture traditionnelle régionale, le confort et la simplicité. Vos hôtes vous proposent: des maisons de campagne agréables en parfaite conformité avec les normes hôtelières.

plusieurs	*several*	la maison	*house*
d'autrefois	*old-style*	la ferme	*farm*

getting around

by public transport

- buying tickets
- enquiring about times and platforms

by road

- buying petrol and other services
- getting breakdown assistance
- taking a taxi

by public transport

buying tickets

 Railway Station 1

Je voudrais un carnet, s'il vous plaît.

A pack of ten underground tickets, please.

Je voudrais un aller-retour **pour** Nantes, s'il vous plaît.

I'd like a return ticket to Nantes, please.

– Vous rentrez quand?

– When are you coming back?

Dimanche soir.

On Sunday evening.

Je rentre le dix-huit juillet.

I'm coming back on July 18th.

Première/seconde classe.

First/second class.

Ça fait combien?

How much is it?

Remember that when you say the date in French, you use **le** plus the ordinal number (for example, *twenty* rather than *twentieth*) plus the month. So, *the tenth of March* is **le dix mars**. The only exception to this rule is for the first of the month. This is expressed as it would be in English: **le premier mars** *the first of March*. The months in French are not written with a capital letter. *(For more help on dates, have a look at the Basics section of the CD-ROM.)*

key vocabulary – public transport

la gare	station
le billet, le ticket, le titre de transport	ticket
la billetterie automatique	self-service ticket machine
les guichets (m)	ticket office
composter	to punch (your ticket to validate it)
un horaire	timetable
la correspondance	connection
sans correspondance	direct, without the need to change
fumeur/non-fumeur	smoking/non-smoking
la sortie	exit
les consignes automatiques (f)	left-luggage lockers
la salle d'attente	waiting room

▣▣▣ enquiring about times and platforms

 Railway Station 1

Le prochain train pour Bordeaux **est à quelle heure?**	*What time is the next train to Bordeaux?*
– Vous avez un train qui quitte Nantes à 18h00 (dix-huit heures).	*– You have a train leaving Nantes at 18.00.*
Le prochain train **part** bien **à** 13h07 (treize heures sept)?	*The next train leaves at 13.07, doesn't it?*
Le train de Rennes **arrive à quelle heure?**	*What time does the train from Rennes arrive?*
Vous pouvez m'indiquer le quai, s'il vous plaît?	*Can you tell me which platform, please?*
– Il faut regarder le tableau.	*– You need to look at the board.*

The key word for talking about time is **heure** *hour*, so asking *what time?* is literally *at what hour?* **à quelle heure?** The answer **à dix heures** *at ten o'clock* is literally *at ten hours. (For more help on time, have a look at the Basics section on the CD-ROM.)*

have a go

1 going underground

You're planning a trip to Canada to visit Montreal with some friends and have decided to use the Metro as much as possible to get around. You've found some information on the internet.

▶ a. What types of ticket can you buy?

b. Does the Metro run during the night?

c. What must you do to your tourist ticket before it is valid for use?

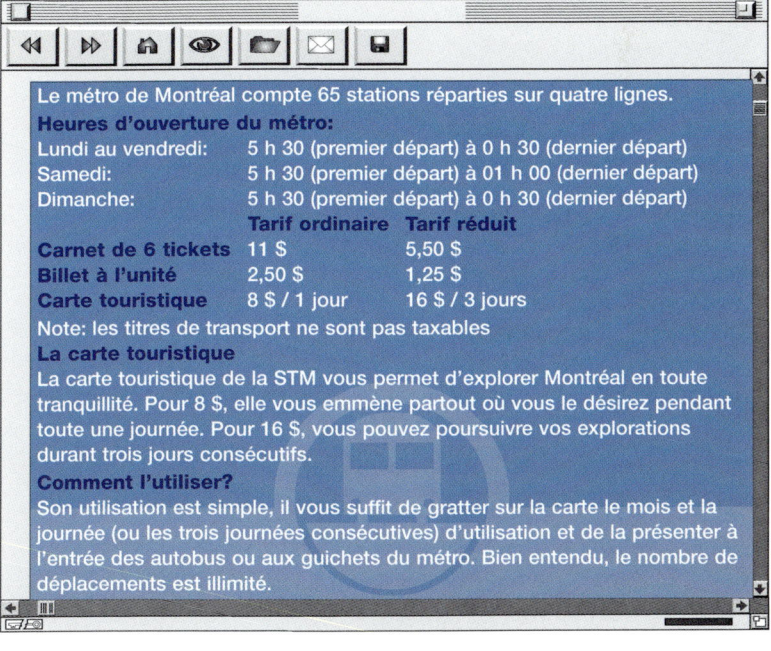

Le métro de Montréal compte 65 stations réparties sur quatre lignes.

Heures d'ouverture du métro:

Lundi au vendredi:	5 h 30 (premier départ) à 0 h 30 (dernier départ)
Samedi:	5 h 30 (premier départ) à 01 h 00 (dernier départ)
Dimanche:	5 h 30 (premier départ) à 0 h 30 (dernier départ)

	Tarif ordinaire	Tarif réduit
Carnet de 6 tickets	11 $	5,50 $
Billet à l'unité	2,50 $	1,25 $
Carte touristique	8 $ / 1 jour	16 $ / 3 jours

Note: les titres de transport ne sont pas taxables

La carte touristique

La carte touristique de la STM vous permet d'explorer Montréal en toute tranquillité. Pour 8 $, elle vous emmène partout où vous le désirez pendant toute une journée. Pour 16 $, vous pouvez poursuivre vos explorations durant trois jours consécutifs.

Comment l'utiliser?

Son utilisation est simple, il vous suffit de gratter sur la carte le mois et la journée (ou les trois journées consécutives) d'utilisation et de la présenter à l'entrée des autobus ou aux guichets du métro. Bien entendu, le nombre de déplacements est illimité.

le billet à l'unité	*single/one ticket*
toute une journée	*a whole day*
comment l'utiliser?	*how do you use it?*
gratter	*to scratch*
le guichet du métro	*metro ticket office*

❯ by road

🟨🟧🟧 buying petrol and other services

Petrol Station 1

Le plein de sans plomb, s'il vous plaît.	*Fill it up with unleaded, please.*
Je peux avoir vingt euros de gazole?	*Can I have twenty euros of diesel?*
Où est-ce que je peux vérifier la pression des pneus?	*Where can I check the tyre pressure?*
Je vous dois combien?	*How much do I owe you?*
Je peux régler par carte de crédit?	*Can I pay by credit card?*

The most straightforward ways of asking questions involving **où** *where*, and **combien** *how much* are: (a) to put **où** and **combien** at the end, for example **Vous allez où?** *Where are you going?* **Je vous dois combien?** *How much do I owe you?* or (b) to use **est-ce que**, for example **Où est-ce que vous allez?** *Where are you going?* **Combien est-ce que je vous dois?** *How much do I owe you? (For more on asking questions, see page 136.)*

🟨🟧🟧 getting breakdown assistance

Petrol Station 2

Je viens de tomber en panne.	*I've just broken down.*
Ma voiture **ne démarre pas.**	*My car won't start.*
Il y a un problème avec les freins.	*There is a problem with the brakes.*
Vous pouvez envoyer une dépanneuse?	*Can you send a breakdown truck?*
Je vous donne le numéro d'immatriculation?	*Shall I give you the registration number?*
– C'est quoi comme voiture?	*– What sort of car is it?*
C'est une Polo noire.	*It's a black Polo.*
– Vous êtes garé où?	*– Where are you parked?*
Sur la route de Condé, **en face du** supermarché.	*On the road to Condé, opposite the supermarket.*

To say that you have just done something, use the present tense of **venir** followed by **de** and an infinitive: <u>**Je viens de** tomber en panne</u> *I've just broken down,* <u>**Je viens d'**arriver</u> *I've just arrived.*

Tips on remembering gender

It can be difficult remembering whether a noun takes **le** or **la**, as it seems so arbitrary. However, there are some useful tips that can help you remember which it is:

Nouns ending in **-euse**, **-ence** and **-tion** are always feminine:

la dépanneuse	*breakdown truck*
l'essence (f)	*petrol*
la direction	*direction*

Makes and models of cars are always feminine because it's **la voiture**:

une Polo noire	*a black Polo*
une Fiat blanche	*a white Fiat*

Nouns ending in **-ment** are masculine, as are nearly all two-syllable or longer words ending in **-eau** and **-age**:

le renseignement	*piece of information*
le remplacement	*replacement*
le panneau	*road sign*
le tableau	*board*
le dépannage	*breakdown service*
le garage	*garage*

Nouns taken from English are usually masculine, as are hyphenated nouns:

le football	*football*
le week-end	*weekend*
le rendez-vous	*meeting, appointment*
le pare-brise	*windscreen*

have a go

▶ You drive up to your guesthouse and are looking for a place to park your car. You notice this sign on a closed gate. Can you park there?

▶ You're driving in France and come across the following sign. What do you have to do?

have a go

roadside rescue

On a touring holiday in Provence, you break down on a country road. Fortunately, you spot this poster on a wall at the side of the road advertising a garage in the next town.

GARAGE SAINT CYR
À votre service depuis 1970

Agent Peugeot

Nos Prestations
- dépannage 24h/24
- recherche véhicule
- entretien et réparation véhicules toutes marques - mécanique, électricité

▶ Will they come and get your car?

▶ Once at the garage, how would you ask them to fill your car up with unleaded fuel and check your tyre pressure?

la voiture	car
les feux (m)	traffic lights
le carrefour	crossroads
le rond-point	roundabout
le parking, le parc de stationnement	car park
stationner	to park
défense de stationner	no parking
la station-service	service station
l'autoroute (f)	motorway
la circulation	traffic
le contractuel	traffic warden
le parcmètre, le parcomètre	parking meter
hors service	out of service, not in use
un embouteillage	traffic jam
la station de taxis	taxi rank
Gardez la monnaie!	Keep the change!

taking a taxi

Petrol Station 4; Hotel 4

Est-ce que vous pouvez m'appeler un taxi **pour aller à** l'aéroport, s'il vous plaît?	*Could you call me a taxi to go to the airport, please?*
Est-ce que vous pourriez m'emmener à la gare?	*Could you take me to the station?*
Ça fait combien?	*How much is it?*
Je peux avoir un reçu?	*Can I have a receipt, please?*
Rendez-moi deux euros, s'il vous plaît.	*Give me back two euros, please.*

When you're asking someone to do something for you, you can either use **pouvez** *can* or **pourriez**, which is the more polite *could*. For example, **Vous pouvez m'aider?** *Can you help me?* or **Vous pourriez m'aider?** *Could you help me?* Both are from **pouvoir** meaning *can* or *to be able to*.

have a go

4 taxi tales

You're coming to the end of your holiday in Annecy and want to book a taxi for Saturday evening at 8pm to take you to Geneva airport. Your hotel gives you this information leaflet about a local taxi service they recommend.

▶ Can you work out the answers to the following questions?

a. What's the price for four people for the time you want?

b. You are a family of five. Can you all go in one taxi?

c. What special offer is the company running at the moment?

ALPHA TAXI

Destinations et tarifs pour la prise en charge de quatre personnes
(pour les cinquième et sixième personnes, nous consulter)

Parcours	Distance (en KM)	De 8h à 19h	De 19h à 8h, dimanches et jours fériés français
Annecy - Aéroport de Chambéry	45	63 EUR	78 EUR
Annecy - Aéroport de Saint-Exupéry (Lyon)	120	156 EUR	168 EUR
Annecy - Aéroport de Genève	45	70 EUR	90 EUR

Promotion du mois: bagages gratuits

Tel. 33 (0)6 07 67 28 83

UNIT 5

asking the way

asking directions

understanding the answer

- in a building
- out and about

on the underground

asking directions

Petrol Station 3; Campsite 3;
Railway Station 4; Department Store 1

Où sont les toilettes?	*Where are the toilets?*
Où se trouve le musée?	*Where is the museum?*
C'est où le commissariat le plus proche?	*Where is the nearest police station?*
Excusez-moi, je cherche le rayon des jouets.	*Excuse me, I'm looking for the toy department.*
Vous savez où je peux acheter des timbres?	*Do you know where I can buy some stamps?*
Vous pouvez m'indiquer où est l'ascenseur?	*Can you tell me where the lift is?*
Pour aller à la plage, s'il vous plaît?	*How do I get to the beach?*

A perfectly polite way of asking for directions is to say **pour aller à** followed by the place you're looking for and **s'il vous plaît.**

Pour aller à la rue de Metz, s'il vous plaît?	*How do I get to Metz Street?*
Pour aller à l'hôtel, s'il vous plaît?	*How do I get to the hotel?*

Remember **à** cannot be followed by **le** or **les**; the words combine to give **au** and **aux** respectively.

Pour aller au marché aux fleurs?	*How do I get to the flower market?*
Pour aller aux Tuileries?	*How do I get to the Tuileries?*

Proche *near* goes after the noun: **un commissariat proche** *a nearby police station. Nearer* is **plus proche** and *nearest* is **le plus proche** when talking about a masculine word and **la plus proche** when talking about a feminine word: **le commissariat le plus proche** *the nearest police station,* **la poste la plus proche** *the nearest post office.*

If you need more precise directions, you could ask the following:

 Department Store 1, 2

C'est où exactement?	*Where is it exactly?*
C'est loin d'ici?	*Is it far from here?*
Ça va me prendre longtemps?	*Is it going to take me long?*
– Ça va vous prendre quelques minutes.	*– It's going to take you a few minutes.*
Vous pouvez m'indiquer la route?	*Can you tell me how to get there?*

One of the simplest ways to talk about the future is to use the present tense of **aller**, just as you can in English: **Je vais...** *I am going to...* and here, **Ça va**... *It is going to...* Verbs following **aller** are always in the infinitive, for example **Je vais <u>prendre</u> le train** *I am going <u>to take</u> the train.*

The pronouns **me** and **vous** (*me, you*) go before the infinitive. For example **Ça va <u>me</u> prendre longtemps?** and **Ça va <u>vous</u> prendre quelques minutes** *(For more on expressing the future, see Unit 10 or the grammar section on page 133.)*

key vocabulary – where things are

derrière	*behind*
devant	*in front of*
là-bas	*over there*
entre	*between*
après	*after*
avant	*before*
à côté (de)	*next (to)*
près (de)	*near (to)*
en face (de)	*opposite*
au bout (de)	*at the end (of)*
à gauche (de)	*to/on the left (of)*
à droite (de)	*to/on the right (of)*
loin de	*far from*

have a go

streets ahead

You're a great puzzle fan, so you buy a puzzle magazine to help improve your French. You recognise the vocabulary in this logic puzzle, so decide to have a go.

▶ Can you work out where the Chinese restaurant is?

▶ What are squares 1 and 7?

▶ One square is not identified – which one is it?

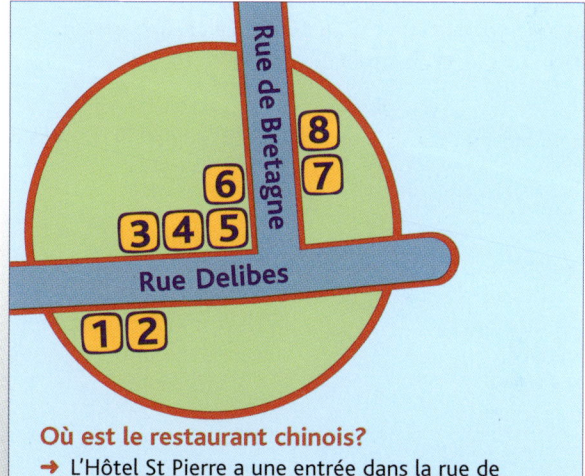

Où est le restaurant chinois?
➔ L'Hôtel St Pierre a une entrée dans la rue de Bretagne et une entrée dans la rue Delibes.
➔ Le Palais de Justice est à côté de l'Hôtel St Pierre dans la rue de Bretagne, en face du musée.
➔ Le supermarché est à côté de l'Hôtel St Pierre.
➔ Le cinéma se trouve à côté du supermarché.
➔ Le Resto Mingo Ho se trouve en face du cinéma et à côté de la poste.

❯ understanding the answer

🟨🟥🟥 in a building

Department Store 1

– C'est au deuxième étage.
– It's on the second floor.

– C'est près de l'entrée.
– It's near the entrance.

– Vous pouvez prendre l'escalier roulant.
– You can take the escalator.

– Vous pouvez prendre l'ascenseur.
– You can take the lift.

– C'est à droite du rayon femmes.
– It's on the right of the ladies' department.

– C'est à gauche de la cafétéria.
– It's on the left of the cafeteria.

– C'est à côté du rayon livres.
– It's next to the book department.

– C'est au bout du couloir.
– It's at the end of the corridor.

Take care with prepositions ending in **de**, such as **près de**, **à côté de**, **à gauche/droite**, **au bout de**. **De** can be followed by **l'** and **la** but not by **le** or **les** – the words combine to give **du** or **des** respectively.

près de l'entrée · near the entrance
en face de la gare · opposite the station
But...
près du rayon musique · near the music department
en face du magasin · opposite the shop
à côté des toilettes · next to the toilets

key vocabulary – in the department store

au sous-sol · in the basement
au rez-de-chaussée · on the ground floor
au premier étage · on the first floor
au deuxième étage · on the second floor
au troisième étage · on the third floor
au quatrième étage · on the fourth floor
au cinquième étage · on the fifth floor

 **out and about**

Campsite 3

– Vous tournez à gauche/à droite.	– *You turn left/right.*
– Vous sortez du camping.	– *You go out of the campsite.*
– Vous traversez la rue/le pont.	– *You cross the road/bridge.*
– Vous prenez la première/ deuxième rue à gauche.	– *You take the first/second road on the left.*
– Vous prenez la direction de Bordeaux.	– *You go in the direction of Bordeaux.*
– Allez tout droit.	– *Go straight ahead.*
– Allez jusqu'au bout de la rue.	– *Go to the end of the road.*
– Continuez tout droit après les feux.	– *Keep going straight on after the traffic lights.*

As you can see from these examples, there are two ways of giving directions or telling someone to do something. One is just to use the **vous** form of the present tense of the verb:

<u>Vous sortez</u> du camping. *You go out of the campsite.*

Alternatively, you can use the **vous** part of the present tense, but without the word **vous**. This is called the imperative.

<u>Continuez</u> tout droit. *Go straight on.*

(You can find more on the imperative in the grammar section on page 135.)

Notice also that **droit** means *straight on* and that it sounds very different from **droite** *right*, where the final **t** is pronounced because it is followed by an **e**.

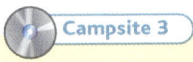

– C'est à dix minutes à pied.	– It's ten minutes' walk.
– C'est à quinze kilomètres d'ici.	– It's 15 kilometres away from here.
– là-bas	– over there
– à côté de la station-service	– next to the petrol station
– près de la gare	– near the station
– en face de l'hôtel de ville	– opposite the town hall
– C'est indiqué.	– It's signposted.

À droite and **à gauche** mean both <u>on</u> *the right/left* and <u>to</u> *the right/left.* These phrases never change. Other similar set phrases include **à pied** *on foot*, **à (dix) minutes à pied** *(ten) minutes' walk*, and **à côté de** *next to, very near. (You can find more on expressions using **à** in the grammar section on page 122.)*

key vocabulary – around town

le carrefour	crossroads, junction
les feux (de signalisation)	traffic lights
le rond-point	roundabout
le coin, au coin	corner, on the corner
le passage pour piétons	pedestrian crossing
le passage souterrain	subway
passer	to go past
l'église (f)	church
le cinéma	cinema
l'école (f)	school
l'hôpital (m)	hospital
la rivière, le fleuve	river

have a go

2 way to go

You've made an arrangement to see a friend for lunch. She's working today, so you're going to meet her at her office. Here are the directions she's sent you by e-mail on how to find her office.

▶ Which landmark are you to look out for when you come out of the metro?

▶ What do you do when you get to this landmark?

▶ Then which way do you turn and what do you look out for?

▶ How will you know when you've reached your friend's office?

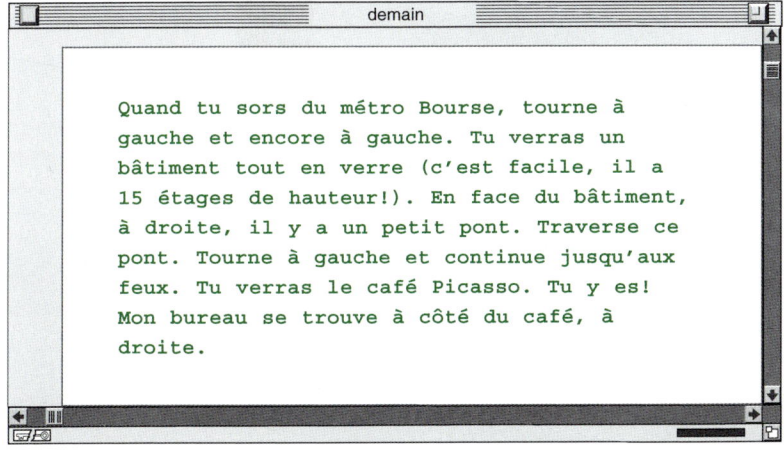

| demain |

> Quand tu sors du métro Bourse, tourne à
> gauche et encore à gauche. Tu verras un
> bâtiment tout en verre (c'est facile, il a
> 15 étages de hauteur!). En face du bâtiment,
> à droite, il y a un petit pont. Traverse ce
> pont. Tourne à gauche et continue jusqu'aux
> feux. Tu verras le café Picasso. Tu y es!
> Mon bureau se trouve à côté du café, à
> droite.

le bâtiment	*building*
tu verras	*you'll see*
la hauteur	*height*
traverser	*to cross*
Tu y es.	*You're there.*

have a go

You're driving to a European Cup football match and have found these directions on the ground's website.

▶ Make some notes in English so that your partner can navigate you along the route while you're driving.

▶ How many roundabouts are there between the motorway and the stadium?

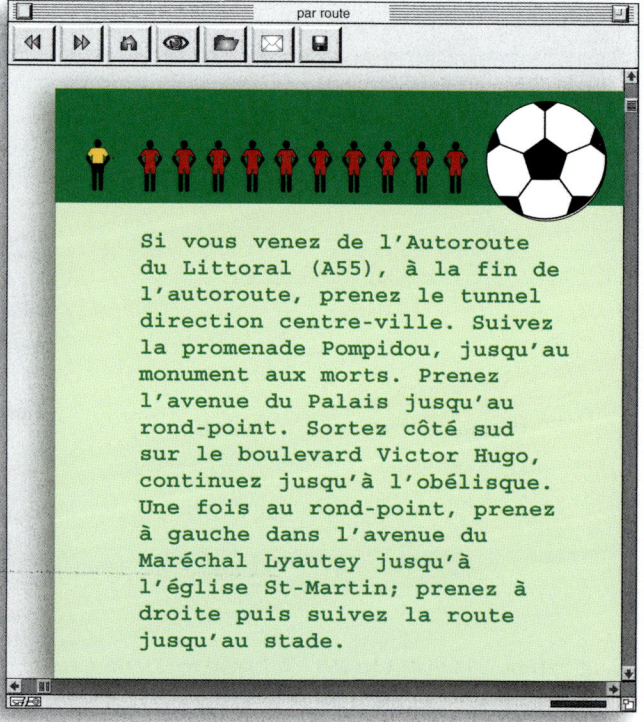

par route

Si vous venez de l'Autoroute
du Littoral (A55), à la fin de
l'autoroute, prenez le tunnel
direction centre-ville. Suivez
la promenade Pompidou, jusqu'au
monument aux morts. Prenez
l'avenue du Palais jusqu'au
rond-point. Sortez côté sud
sur le boulevard Victor Hugo,
continuez jusqu'à l'obélisque.
Une fois au rond-point, prenez
à gauche dans l'avenue du
Maréchal Lyautey jusqu'à
l'église St-Martin; prenez à
droite puis suivez la route
jusqu'au stade.

l'autoroute (f)	*motorway*
le sud	*south*
le stade	*stadium*

❯ on the underground

 Railway Station 3

C'est quelle direction pour aller à Jussieu?	*What direction is it to go to Jussieu?*
À Odéon, **il faut prendre quelle ligne?**	*Which line do I have to take at Odéon?*
Il faut prendre quelle ligne pour aller à Concorde?	*Which line do I have to take to get to Concorde?*
Il faut changer à quelle station?	*Which station do I need to change at?*
Il faut descendre à quelle station pour aller à la Tour Eiffel?	*Which station do I need to get off at for the Eiffel Tower?*

The French for *what?* or *which?*, when you mean *which one out of several?* is **quel?** This has masculine and feminine forms.

Quel quai? (le quai)   *Which platform?*
Quelle ligne? (la ligne)   *Which line?*

Although the spelling of **quel(le)** changes, the pronunciation stays the same.

 Railway Station 3

– Il faut changer à Odéon.	– *You have to change at Odéon.*
– Il faut prendre la ligne 4 direction Porte d'Orléans.	– *You have to take line 4 in the direction of Porte d'Orléans.*
– À Odéon vous prenez la ligne 10.	– *At Odeon you take line 10.*
– Vous descendez à Bir-Hakeim.	– *Get off at Bir-Hakeim.*

Notice **il faut** can be used both to ask *Do I have to...?* and to reply *You have to...* Think of it as meaning *It is necessary (to)* to help you remember how it works. The verb following **il faut** is always in the infinitive. (*You can find more on using* **il faut** *in the grammar section on page 135.*)

sightseeing and leisure

exploring in town

- finding out about places of interest
- checking opening times

at the campsite or beach

- enquiring about activities

exploring in town

 finding out about places of interest

Railway Station 2

– Je peux vous renseigner?
**Je voudrais des renseignements
sur** le musée.
– Je vais vous donner ce dépliant.
Vous pouvez me donner un plan
de la ville, s'il vous plaît?

*– Can I help you?
I'd like some information about
the museum.
– I'll give you this brochure.
Can you give me a map of the
town, please?*

Information is plural in French, unlike in English: **des renseignements**.
The singular **un renseignement** has the specific meaning of a single item
of information. And although in English we ask for information *about* or
on something, French only uses **sur** *on*.

In the phrases **Je vais vous donner...** and **Vous pouvez me donner...**,
the **vous** and the **me** mean *to you* and *to me.* In English, you can miss
out the word 'to', as in *You can give me...* but we do say *give something to
someone.* Object pronouns (such as **vous** and **me** in the phrases above)
go before the verb in French. Where there is a verb followed by an
infinitive (as in the two phrases above), they go directly before the
infinitive: **Vous pouvez me donner...**, **Je peux vous donner...** *(You can find
more on these indirect object pronouns in the grammar section on page 119.)*

Campsite 3

Qu'est-ce qu'il y a à voir dans
la région?
Qu'est-ce qu'il y a à visiter dans
la ville?

*What is there to see in the
region?
What is there to visit in the town?*

When you're asking about what there is to do in a place, the French
expression **Qu'est-ce qu'il y a...?** *What is there...?* takes **à** before the verb:
Qu'est-ce qu'il y a à voir? *What is there to see?* Just learn it as a set phrase
and add on the verb you need. So, for example, *What is there to do?*
would be **Qu'est-ce qu'il y a à faire?**

le musée	*museum*
le musée d'art	*art gallery*
le zoo	*zoo*
la cathédrale	*cathedral*
le château	*castle*
le vignoble	*vineyard*
le stade	*stadium*
le marché aux puces	*flea-market*
le jardin botanique	*botanic garden*
le palais	*palace*
la tour	*tower*
l'exposition (f)	*exhibition*

checking opening times

Railway Station 2

Quelles sont les heures d'ouverture?	*What are the opening times?*
Le château **est ouvert** aujourd'hui?	*Is the castle open today?*
– Le musée **est fermé** le lundi.	*– The museum is closed on Mondays.*
Il/elle ferme à quelle heure?	*What time does it close?*
Il/elle ouvre à quelle heure le matin?	*What time does it open in the morning?*
– Il/elle ouvre de dix heures à dix-huit heures.	*– It's open from 10a. until 6pm (18.00).*

Lundi and **le lundi** have different meanings. The **le** shows that you are referring to *every* Monday or Mondays in general. Without **le** it means one specific Monday or *on Monday*.

Dimanche je vais au musée.	*On Sunday I'm going to the museum (ie one particular occasion).*
Le dimanche je vais à l'église.	*On Sundays I go to church (ie every Sunday).*

have a go

1 cartoon culture

You and a friend are in Brussels for a short break. It's Monday evening and you plan to stay until Thursday. There's an information brochure in your hotel room about some of the city's many museums.

▶ Which ones will it be possible for you to visit over the next two days?

▶ You know your friend is a great fan of the Belgian cartoon character Tintin. Which museum would particularly interest him and why?

Musée de l'Eau et de la Fontaine
Une exposition permanente consacrée à l'eau et aux fontaines.
Musée de l'Eau et de la Fontaine, avenue Hoover, 63, 1332 Genval.
Ouvert tous les week-ends et jours fériés de 10 à 18h, en semaine sur rendez-vous pour les groupes (au minimum 20 personnes).

Le Clockarium
Un musée consacré uniquement aux horloges en faïence.
Clockarium, 163 bd Reyers, B -1030 Bruxelles.
Ouvert tous les jours sauf dimanches et jours fériés à 10h30, pour des visites guidées d'environ 1h20.

Musée d'Art Fantastique (MAF)
Des expositions permanentes et temporaires des œuvres surréalistes et bizarres.
Musée d'Art Fantastique, 7 rue Américaine, 1060 Bruxelles.
Ouvert mardi - samedi, de 12 à 17h.

Centre Belge de la Bande Dessinée
Musée consacré aux bandes dessinées, avec une attention spéciale accordée aux dessins de Hergé.
Centre Belge de la Bande Dessinée, 20 rue des Sables, 1000 Bruxelles.
Horaire: tous les jours, sauf le lundi, de 10h à 18h.

la faïence	*earthenware*
la bande dessinée	*cartoon*
les jours fériés (m)	*bank holidays*

enquiring about activities

 Campsite 1, 2

Qu'est-ce qu'on peut faire comme activités?
– Vous pouvez utiliser la piscine, jouer au tennis.
Quels sports nautiques **est-ce qu'on peut faire** ici?
– Vous pouvez faire de la plongée sous-marine, du jet-ski.

What sort of activities can you do?
– You can use the swimming pool, play tennis.
Which water sports can you do here?
– You can go scuba-diving, jet-skiing.

English has lots of sporty verbs, for example *to windsurf, to jet-ski, to scuba-dive.* French tends to use phrases instead, many of them starting with **faire** *to do.* You are literally saying *do some windsurfing, do some diving* and so on. Remember that the word for *some* will change depending on the gender of the noun.

faire du jet-ski
  (<u>le</u> ski)   *to jet-ski*
faire de la planche à voile
  (<u>la</u> planche à voile)   *to windsurf*
faire de l'escalade
  (begins with a <u>vowel</u>)   *to go climbing*
faire des sports nautiques
  (<u>plural</u>)   *to do water sports*

Quel? means *what?* or *which?* in the sense of *which one of several?* and is always accompanied by a noun. Because **quel** is an adjective, it has different forms for masculine, feminine, singular and plural. (*You can find more on* **quel** *in the grammar section on page 137.*)

Vous préférez <u>quel</u> sport nautique?   *Which water sport do you prefer?*
À <u>quelle</u> heure?   *At what time?*
<u>Quels</u> sports nautiques est-ce qu'on peut faire ici?   *Which water sports can you do here?*
<u>Quelles</u> sont les heures d'ouverture?   *What are the opening times?*

 Campsite 1, 2

On peut faire des sports nautiques ici?	*Is it possible to do water sports here?*
On peut prendre des cours de plongée?	*Is it possible to take diving lessons?*
On peut louer les planches à voile?	*Is it possible to hire windsurf boards?*
C'est combien la location?	*How much does it cost to rent?*
– C'est treize euros de l'heure.	*– It's 13 euros per hour.*
– Il faut payer une caution de vingt euros.	*– You have to pay a deposit of 20 euros.*
Je peux réserver pour demain?	*Can I book for tomorrow?*

On peut from the verb **pouvoir**, has the general meaning *Is it possible? Can you?* It is nearly always followed by another verb – the activity you are asking about – and this verb is in the infinitive form. For example, **On peut faire du jet-ski?** *Is it possible to jet-ski?* **Je peux...**, also from **pouvoir**, behaves in the same way: **Je peux réserver pour onze heures?** *Can I book for 11 o'clock?*

key vocabulary – sporting activities

faire de la voile	*to go sailing*
faire du vélo tout terrain (VTT)	*to go mountain biking*
faire du tir à l'arc	*to do archery*
faire de l'escalade (f)	*to go climbing*
faire du canoë-kayak	*to go canoeing*
faire du ski nautique	*to water-ski*
aller à la pêche	*to fish*
jouer au mini-golf	*to play crazy golf*
faire du patinage	*to ice-skate*
faire du skateboard	*to skateboard*
faire du snowboard	*to snowboard*
faire du roller	*to go roller blading*
faire du patin à roulettes	*to go roller skating*
faire de l'équitation (f)	*to go horseriding*

have a go

2 | life's a beach club

You and three friends want to go to a beach club in the Basque region of France. Kim wants a place that offers water sports, Chris would like to explore the surrounding countryside on a bike, Jordan wants a gym or fitness centre on site and you'd like a taste of Basque culture.

▶ a. Make a list of the water sports on offer at the various clubs.
  b. Which clubs have both bike hire and a gym?
  c. Which of the beach clubs below would best satisfy everyone?
  d. If you went to that club, what other activities could you do?

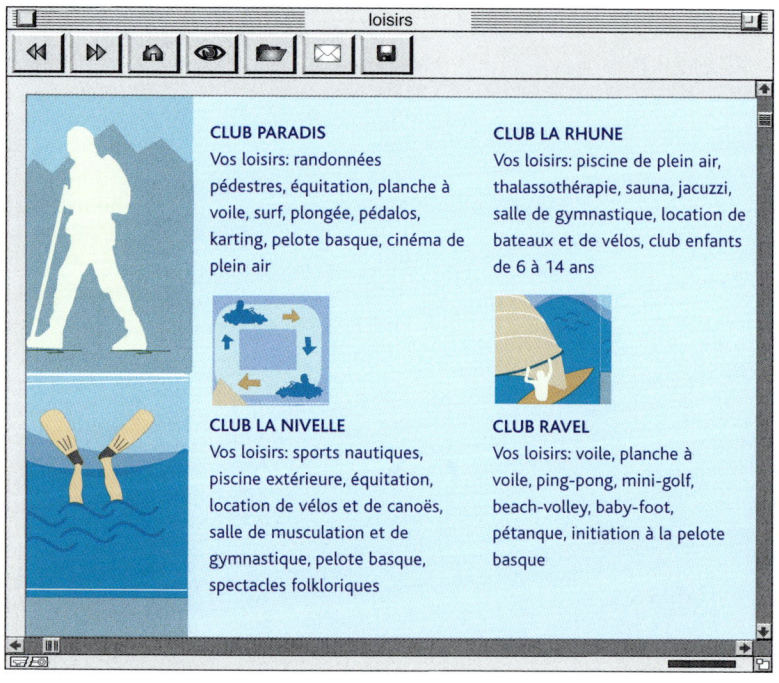

loisirs

CLUB PARADIS
Vos loisirs: randonnées pédestres, équitation, planche à voile, surf, plongée, pédalos, karting, pelote basque, cinéma de plein air

CLUB LA RHUNE
Vos loisirs: piscine de plein air, thalassothérapie, sauna, jacuzzi, salle de gymnastique, location de bateaux et de vélos, club enfants de 6 à 14 ans

CLUB LA NIVELLE
Vos loisirs: sports nautiques, piscine extérieure, équitation, location de vélos et de canoës, salle de musculation et de gymnastique, pelote basque, spectacles folkloriques

CLUB RAVEL
Vos loisirs: voile, planche à voile, ping-pong, mini-golf, beach-volley, baby-foot, pétanque, initiation à la pelote basque

la salle de musculation	*weights room*
le karting	*go-karting*
le baby-foot	*table football*
la pelote basque	*pelota*
la randonnée pédestre	*walk, hike*

UNIT 7

buying food

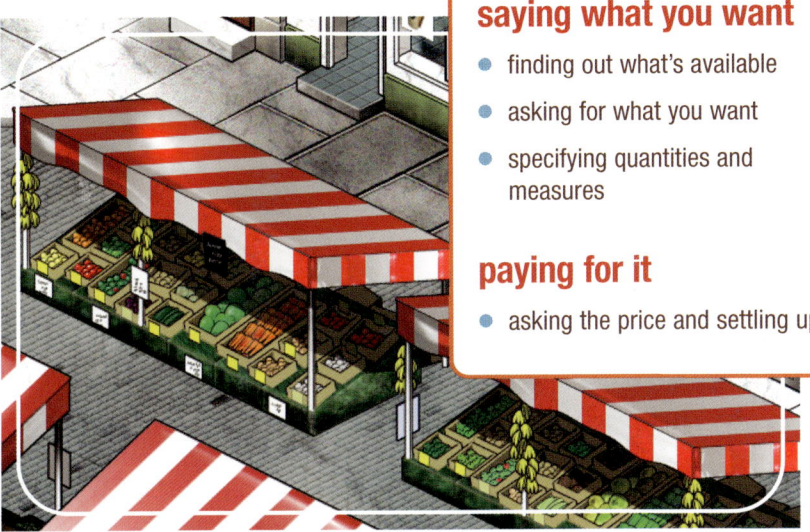

saying what you want

- finding out what's available
- asking for what you want
- specifying quantities and measures

paying for it

- asking the price and settling up

saying what you want

finding out what's available

 Market Square 2

– Et pour vous... qu'est-ce que ce sera?

Vous avez des champignons?

Qu'est-ce que vous avez comme fromages de la région?

– Nous avons du reblochon, du chèvre ou de la tomme.

Vous pouvez me recommander du saucisson?

– And for you... what will it be?

Do you have any mushrooms?

What types of local cheeses have you got?

– We have Reblochon, goat's cheese or Tomme.

Can you recommend some dried sausage?

Du, de la and **des** *some* or *any* are used when asking about an unspecified quantity of something. They also mean, more literally, *of* or *from the*: **de la région** *from the local area*. Whatever its meaning, **de** cannot be followed by **le** or **les**; instead it combines with them to form **du** and **des** respectively.

key vocabulary – delicatessen

le brie	*Brie*
le chèvre	*goat's cheese*
le roquefort	*Roquefort blue cheese*
le jambon cru	*raw ham*
le jambon cuit	*cooked ham*
le jambon de Parme	*Parma ham*
le parmesan	*Parmesan*
le pâté	*pâté*
le pâté de campagne	*coarse pâté*
le pâté de foie	*liver pâté*
la saucisse	*sausage*
le saucisson sec	*dried sausage*

asking for what you want

Market Square 1, 3

Quatre croissants, s'il vous plaît.	*Four croissants, please.*
Je voudrais une baguette.	*I'd like one baguette.*
Je voudrais aussi du fromage.	*I'd also like some cheese.*
Donnez-moi une livre de fraises.	*Give me a pound of strawberries.*
– Et avec ça?/Et avec ceci?	*– Anything else?*
– Autre chose?/C'est tout?	*– Is that all?*

Je voudrais is a polite way of saying what you want. (**Je veux** *I want* and **Je voudrais** *I would like* both come from the verb **vouloir** *to want*.) Another way is simply to name the item, and follow it with **s'il vous plaît** *please*.

Donnez-moi is slightly more business-like and no-nonsense, but is not impolite like the literal English translation *Give me*. Use this when you're well into your conversation, say, when you're ordering the third or fourth item on your list.

key vocabulary – bakery

le pain	*bread*
le petit pain	*bread roll*
le pain au chocolat	*chocolate-filled croissant*
la brioche	*sweet bun*
la pâtisserie	*cake shop*
les pâtisseries (f)	*pastries*
le gâteau	*cake*
la crème (chantilly)	*(whipped) cream*
la crêpe	*pancake*
la galette	*savoury pancake*
le biscuit	*biscuit*
le beignet	*doughnut*
la gaufre	*waffle*
le sablé	*shortbread*
le millefeuille	*cream slice*
la tarte aux framboises	*raspberry tart*
la tarte aux poires	*pear tart*

have a go

1 which wine?

You want to take home a bottle of wine as a present for a friend.
Your friend doesn't eat meat, but does eat fish. She hasn't got a sweet
tooth. There's a list in the wine shop advising which wine goes with
which dishes.

▶ Which of the bottles on the list would be best for your friend?

▶ Choose a wine to serve with each of the following dishes for a
  special summer dinner:

    a. cold poached salmon
    b. lamb cutlets
    c. strawberries and whipped cream

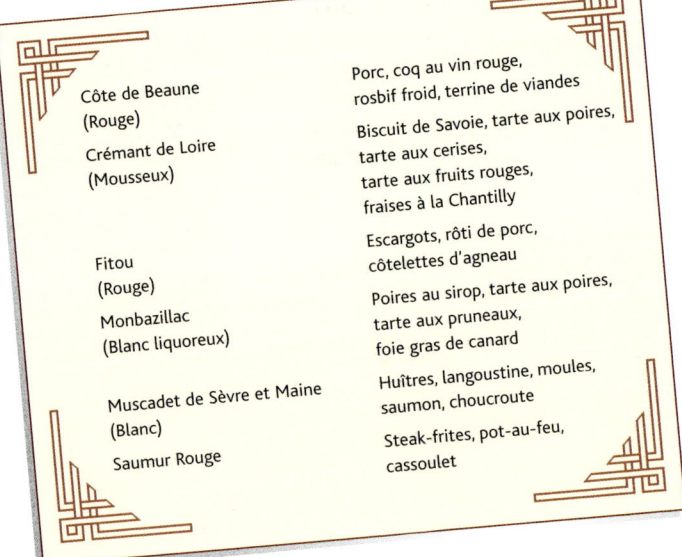

Côte de Beaune
(Rouge)

Crémant de Loire
(Mousseux)

Fitou
(Rouge)

Monbazillac
(Blanc liquoreux)

Muscadet de Sèvre et Maine
(Blanc)

Saumur Rouge

Porc, coq au vin rouge,
rosbif froid, terrine de viandes

Biscuit de Savoie, tarte aux poires,
tarte aux cerises,
tarte aux fruits rouges,
fraises à la Chantilly

Escargots, rôti de porc,
côtelettes d'agneau

Poires au sirop, tarte aux poires,
tarte aux pruneaux,
foie gras de canard

Huîtres, langoustine, moules,
saumon, choucroute

Steak-frites, pot-au-feu,
cassoulet

les escargots (m)   *snails*
les pruneaux (m)   *prunes*
les huîtres (f)   *oysters*

▢▢▢ specifying quantities and measures

 Market Square 1, 2

Trois cents grammes de champignons.	*300 grammes of mushrooms.*
Un kilo de pêches blanches.	*A kilo of white peaches.*
Un bouquet de persil.	*A bunch of parsley.*
Dix tranches de saucisson.	*Ten slices of sausage.*
Une boîte de thon.	*A tin of tuna.*
Un paquet de gruyère râpé.	*A packet of grated Gruyère.*
Un pot de moutarde.	*A jar of mustard.*
Un morceau de fromage.	*A piece of cheese.*
– **Combien de** melons?	*– How many melons?*
Un gros, s'il vous plaît.	*A big one, please.*

Specific quantities, as in English, are all followed by **de** *of*. This includes slices, pieces, packets or jars, and so on, as well as weight or volume. Unlike English, **Combien?** *How much, how many?* is also followed by **de**. As mentioned before, if you do not specify a quantity, then **de** is followed by the appropriate word for *the* – be aware of gender (**le** or **la**) and number (singular or plural). Remember that **de** combines with **le** or **les** to form **du** and **des** respectively.

Vous voulez **du** saucisson à l'ail?	*Do you want some garlic sausage?*
Je voudrais **de la** rhubarbe.	*I'd like some rhubarb.*
Vous avez **des** croissants?	*Have you got any croissants?*

key vocabulary – fruit and veg

la framboise	*raspberry*
la fraise	*strawberry*
la pomme	*apple*
la banane	*banana*
la pastèque	*watermelon*
les raisins (m)	*grapes*
le champignon	*mushroom*
la tomate	*tomato*
le persil	*parsley*
la salade	*salad/lettuce*

have a go

2 just desserts

You've bought a French cookery magazine at a **bureau de tabac** and decide to have a go at making one of the recipes, **clafoutis aux fruits** *fruit pastry*. You're just off to the fruit and vegetable market to buy the fresh ingredients. The recipe is for eight people, but you are making it for your family of four.

▸ Which fruits do you need to buy at the market?

▸ Now imagine you're at the market. What are the phrases you will need in order to ask for the correct quantities of the ingredients for your clafoutis?

Clafoutis aux fruits

Ingrédients
(pour 8 personnes)
500g de pêches
300g de cerises
500g de pommes
150g de farine
200g de sucre
6 œufs
300ml de lait
jus d'un citron
1 pincée de sel
4 cuillères à soupe de
    kirsch ou de rhum
50g de beurre

la farine	*flour*
le sucre	*sugar*
le lait	*milk*
le beurre	*butter*

❯ paying for it

🟨🟧🟥 asking the price and settling up

 Market Square 1, 3

C'est combien les tartes aux fruits?

How much are the fruit tarts?

Les melons, **c'est combien la pièce?**

How much is it for one melon?

– Un cinquante la pièce.

– One euro fifty each.

Les tomates, **c'est combien le kilo?**

How much is a kilo of tomatoes?

– Deux euros vingt le kilo.

– Two euros twenty per kilo.

Ça fait combien?

How much is it altogether?

Excusez-moi, je n'ai pas de monnaie.

Sorry, I haven't got any change.

J'ai seulement un billet de 50 euro.

I've only got a 50 euro note.

C'est combien... can be used when asking about the price of one thing or several; it means both *How much is*...? and *How much are*...?

Notice that **monnaie** means *change*, and that **argent** is the word for *money*:

Je n'ai pas de monnaie. *I haven't got any change.*
Je n'ai pas d'argent. *I haven't got any money.*

have a go

3 money matters

In the supermarket you pick up a packet of grated Emmenthal cheese and a bottle of apple juice. There's a promotional label on each item.

▶ What do they say?

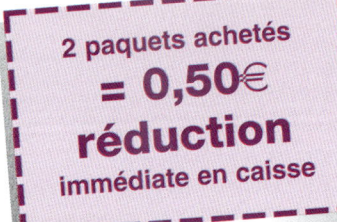

▶ You're queuing at the checkout and suddenly realise that you don't have enough cash on you, though you do have a Visa card and travellers' cheques. There's a notice about methods of payment. How will you pay?

PAIEMENTS ACCEPTÉS
ESPÈCES
CARTES BANCAIRES
CHÈQUES BANCAIRES
CHÈQUES DÉJEUNERS
MASTERCARD
VISA
AMERICAN EXPRESS

acheter	to buy
la moitié	half
espèces (f)	cash
la caisse	till, checkout

UNIT 8

shopping

in a department store

- asking for what you want
- trying things on
- making up your mind

in the chemist's

- explaining what's wrong
- understanding the chemist's advice

in a department store

asking for what you want

 Department Store 1, 2, 3

Vous avez des cartes d'anniversaire?	*Do you have any birthday cards?*
Je voudrais ce vase-là en bleu.	*I'd like that vase in blue.*
Je cherche un chemisier.	*I am looking for a blouse.*
Vous l'avez en noir (**en** quarante)?	*Do you have it in black (in a 40)?*
– Nous avons celui-ci en rouge, noir et ivoire.	– *We have this one in red, black and ivory.*
C'est un peu cher.	*It's a bit expensive.*
– Il y en a de moins chers en coton.	– *There are some cheaper ones in cotton.*

Ce and its feminine form **cette** mean both *this* and *that*. If you've got one vase in your hand and there's another on the shelf, and you say **Je voudrais ce vase**, the assistant won't know which one you mean. To avoid this ambiguity, tag **-ci** on to **vase** to specify *this* and **-là** for *that*.

Je voudrais <u>ce</u> vase-<u>ci</u>.	*I'd like <u>this</u> vase.*
Je voudrais <u>ce</u> vase-<u>là</u>.	*I'd like <u>that</u> vase.*
Je prends <u>cette</u> carte-<u>là</u>.	*I'll take <u>that</u> card.*
Je prends <u>ces</u> gants-<u>là</u>.	*I'll take <u>those</u> gloves.*

(You can find more on how to specify which one or ones you are referring to – using demonstrative adjectives – in the grammar section on page 120.)

key vocabulary – materials

le coton	cotton
la laine	wool
la soie	silk
le cachemire	cashmere
la fourrure	fur
le tricot	jersey, knitted fabric
le cuir	leather
le verre	glass
le bois	wood

Put the word **en** before the above nouns to mean *made out of*: **un T-shirt en coton** *a cotton T-shirt*, **des chaussures en cuir** *leather shoes*, **un vase en verre** *a glass vase*.

key vocabulary – colours

masculine	**feminine**	
noir	noire	black
blanc	blanche	white
vert	verte	green
bleu	bleue	blue
gris	grise	grey
violet	violette	purple
rouge	rouge	red
jaune	jaune	yellow
rose	rose	pink
orange	orange	orange
marron	marron	brown

When these colours refer to plural nouns, add **-s** to the masculine or feminine form as appropriate:

les gants noirs (m) *black gloves*
les chaussures bleues (f) *blue shoes*

Colours that end in **-e** are the same for both masculine and feminine. **Orange** and **marron** never change, even in the plural: **les chaussures marron** *brown shoes*.

have a go

shopping heaven

You've come into a large department store to buy some presents to take home – a computer game for your brother, some perfume for your mother, a CD for your father and a toy for your niece. You also want to buy some postcards, but the first thing you want to do is sit down with a cup of coffee.

▶ Which floors will you visit?

PLAN DU MAGASIN	
6ème étage	Salon de beauté
	Coiffeur
	Service clientèle
	Restaurant gourmet
5ème étage	Papeterie
	Bureautique
	Multimédia – livres,
	informatique, jeux
	PC, CD, DVD, vidéo
4ème étage	Maison
	Déco
	Café-Bar
3ème étage	Enfants –
	mode, loisirs, jouets
2ème étage	Mode femme –
	lingerie, chaussures
1er étage	Mode homme –
	lingerie, chaussures
Rez-de-chaussée	Bijouterie
	Parfumerie
	Bagagerie
	Collants
	Accessoires

trying things on

Department Store 3, 4

Je voudrais essayer ces bottines.	*I'd like to try on these ankle boots.*
Je peux l'essayer?	*Can I try it on?*
Je peux les essayer?	*Can I try them on?*
Je peux essayer les deux?	*Can I try them both on?*
– Oui, bien sûr. Les cabines sont là-bas.	*– Yes, of course. The changing rooms are over there.*
– Vous faites quelle taille?	*– What size are you? (clothes)*
Du 40.	*I'm a 40.*
– Quelle est votre pointure?	*– What size are you? (shoes)*
Je fais du 38.	*I'm a size 38.*

When **le, la, l'** and **les** are before a noun they mean *the.* But when they're before a verb they mean *it* or *them.* The one used depends on what *it* or *them* refers back to: **J'aime <u>le</u> T-shirt noir; je <u>le</u> prends**. *I like the black T-shirt; I'll take it.* **J'aime <u>les</u> gants; je peux <u>les</u> essayer?** *I like the gloves; can I try them on?*

key vocabulary – clothes and shoes

des baskets (f)	*trainers*
des chaussures de sport (f)	*trainers*
des bottes (f)	*boots*
des chaussettes (f)	*socks*
des chaussures (f) (à talons hauts)	*(high-heeled) shoes*
la chemise	*shirt*
le chemisier	*blouse*
la cravate	*tie*
le jean	*jeans*
la jupe (plissée)	*(pleated) skirt*
le manteau	*coat*
le pantalon	*trousers*
le pull	*jumper*
le short	*shorts*
le T-shirt (à manches longues)	*(long-sleeved) T-shirt*
la veste	*jacket*

have a go

You are on holiday in Paris and are thinking about the presents you are going to buy for friends and family back home. This is your list so far:

Meera	*French pop music*
Tom	*French comic book*
Grandma	*Scarf*
Mo	*T-shirt*
Sam and Joe	*Computer games*

As you walk down a shopping street in the centre of Paris you are handed a flyer for a local store.

▶ a. How many presents from your list are you likely to find there?

b. Do they offer a gift-wrapping service?

c. Could you pay with your Diners Card or a credit card?

d. You're not planning to return to your hotel until late in the evening and don't really want to carry your purchases around with you. Would they deliver to your hotel a couple of miles away?

e. You will probably be in this area later in the week. If you bring

---

CHAPITRE PREMIER

Chapitre Premier vous propose un très grand choix de livres, CD, cassettes, vidéos, DVD, logiciels et jeux vidéos. Nous nous spécialisons dans la vente de bandes dessinées - nous avons plus de 2000 titres.

Heures d'ouverture
Lundi – vendredi: 10h00 à 18h00
Samedi: 9h00 à 17h00

Cartes de crédit
Nous acceptons les cartes de crédit suivantes: Eurocard/Mastercard, Visa et American Express.

Service emballage cadeau
Nous pouvons adresser vos commandes sous emballage cadeau pour 1€ de plus par article. Nous emballons individuellement vos cadeaux dans un papier élégant.

Livraison gratuite
Livraison à domicile gratuite à partir de 100€ d'achats. Paris 1er arrondissement.

Parking
Deux heures de parking gratuit à partir de 30€ d'achats.

---

le logiciel	software	l'emballage	wrapping
le jeu vidéo	computer game	emballer	to wrap
la bande dessinée	cartoon	la livraison	delivery

making up your mind

Department Store 2, 3, 4

– Vous aimez celui-ci/celle-ci?	– Do you like this one (m/f)?
J'aime bien le blanc/la blanche.	I like the white one (m/f) very much.
Le rouge est très joli.	The red one (m) is very pretty.
– Ça va?	– How is it? Is it all right?
Oui, **ça va.**	Yes, it fits.
– Vous les prenez?	– Will you take them?
Je vais les prendre en marron.	I'll take them in brown.
Je le/la prends.	I'll take it (m/f).
Ça coûte combien?	How much is it?
– C'est pour offrir?	– Is it a gift?
– Je vous fais un paquet-cadeau?	– Shall I wrap it for you?

J'aime beaucoup la rouge makes it clear that you're talking about a **la** word (feminine) and you don't have to repeat the noun. If you're talking about **le T-shirt** or **le vase**, you say **j'aime beaucoup le rouge**. **J'aime beaucoup les verts** makes it clear you're talking about masculine plural things, eg **les gants** *gloves*; if they were feminine, eg **les chaussures** *shoes*, you would say **j'aime beaucoup les vertes**, with the feminine plural ending.

key vocabulary – accessories

la bague	*ring*
le bonnet	*woolly hat*
la ceinture	*belt*
le chapeau	*hat*
le collier	*necklace*
le foulard	*long scarf*
les gants	*gloves*
les lunettes (de soleil) (f)	*(sun) glasses*
la montre	*watch*
le sac à main	*handbag*

have a go

dream jeans

Your friend has seen some fantastic jeans on sale in the market and asks for your help with the language she needs to go and buy a pair.

▶ Help her prepare the phrases she needs to convey the following basic information (remember jeans are singular in French):

a. She wants a pair of black jeans.

b. She's a size 44.

▶ She's still feeling shy about it, so you go with her to the market and find the jeans stall. She needs to say the following – can you help her out?

c. Can I try these on?

d. How much are they?

e. Yes, that's fine, I'll take them.

> **À saisir!**
> **Jeans et vestes**
> **de haute qualité**
> **à bas prix!**

bas(se)	*low*
haut(e)	*high*

in the chemist's

explaining what's wrong

Market Square 4

Je voudrais quelque chose pour les coups de soleil.	*I'd like something for sunburn.*
J'ai un peu de fièvre.	*I have a slight temperature.*
J'ai mal à la tête.	*I have a headache.*
J'ai mal à l'oreille.	*I have ear-ache.*
J'ai mal aux dents.	*I have toothache.*

Avoir mal à is the phrase to use when you've got a pain or something is sore or aching. It's followed by the part of the body causing the problem. **À** can be followed by **la** and **l'**, but not by **le** or **les**. It combines with these two to form **au** and **aux** respectively: **J'ai mal au ventre** *I've got stomach-ache* (it's **le** ventre), **Vous avez mal aux pieds?** *Are your feet aching?*

key vocabulary – parts of the body

la tête	*head*
l'oreille (f)	*ear*
la gorge	*throat*
les dents (la dent)	*teeth (tooth)*
la jambe	*leg*
le pied	*foot*
le ventre	*stomach*
le dos	*back*
le bras	*arm*
la main	*hand*

 understanding the chemist's advice

Market Square 4

– Je vous conseille cette crème.	– I recommend this cream.
– Prenez ces comprimés deux fois par jour.	– Take these tablets twice a day.
– Il faut aller chez le médecin.	– You must go to the doctor's.

When the chemist gives instructions, she or he uses the imperative. This is the **vous** form of the verb, but without the word **vous.** So, instead of **vous prenez** *you take*, you'll hear **prenez** *take*. For example, **Prenez ces comprimés** *Take these tablets.*

In printed instructions, such as those on medicine packets, the infinitive of the verb is often used instead of the imperative, so you will see **Avaler le comprimé avec un grand verre d'eau** *Swallow the tablet with a large glass of water.* Similarly, in a recipe, you will see **Ajouter les échalotes, mélanger délicatement** *Add the shallots, mix gently. (You can find more on the imperative in the grammar section on page 135).*

Notice the striking similarities between the following:

ces comprimés	*these pills*
les comprimés	*the pills*
des comprimés	*some pills*
mes comprimés	*my pills*
ses comprimés	*his, her pills*

Look out for patterns like this in French. Once you've learnt **les**, for instance, you'll have no trouble recognising other plurals.

key vocabulary – ailments

Je me sens mal	*I don't feel well*
la fièvre	*a temperature*
la grippe	*flu*
la gueule de bois	*a hangover*
J'ai la nausée	*I feel sick*
le rhume	*a cold*

have a go

teething troubles

Disaster has struck while you're on holiday, in the form of a bad toothache. You decide you can't face the dentist, so you go to the chemist's, where you are sold some tablets.

▶ Read the instruction leaflet below.

a. When and how should you take the tablets?

b. What's the maximum daily dosage?

c. You're currently taking a course of antibiotics after a bout of the flu, can you take these tablets?

d. Your 13-year-old daughter, who is asthmatic, has a headache and asks for one of your tablets. Are the tablets suitable for this problem and can she have one?

Cal-Med

Ce médicament contient un anti-inflammatoire non stéroïdien: l'ibuprofène. Il est indiqué chez l'adulte et l'enfant de plus de 12 ans dans le traitement de la fièvre, du mal de tête ou de dents et de la grippe.

Ce médicament NE DOIT PAS ÊTRE UTILISÉ dans les cas suivants:
à partir du 5ème mois de grossesse
antécédent d'allergie aux autres anti-inflammatoires non stéroïdiens ou à l'aspirine
antécédent d'asthme
ulcère de l'estomac

COMMENT UTILISER CE MÉDICAMENT
1 comprimé (200 mg), à renouveler si besoin au bout de 4 heures
Ne pas dépasser 6 comprimés par jour (soit 1200 mg par jour)

MODE D'ADMINISTRATION
Voie orale. Avaler le comprimé avec un grand verre d'eau, de préférence au cours d'un repas.

		ne pas depasser	*do not exceed*
la grossesse	*pregnancy*	renouveler	*repeat*
un repas	*meal*	si besoin	*if necessary*

chatting and socialising

talking about your interests

- expressing likes and dislikes

making arrangements

- inviting someone to do something
- accepting an invitation

❯ talking about your interests

🔲🔲🔲 expressing likes and dislikes

 **Bar 3**

J'aime le cinéma.	*I like the cinema.*
J'aime bien aller au théâtre.	*I really like going to the theatre.*
J'adore les concerts de rock.	*I love rock concerts.*
Je n'aime pas danser.	*I don't like dancing.*
Je n'aime pas trop le Bar du Soleil.	*I don't really like the Bar du Soleil.*
Je déteste la musique classique.	*I hate classical music.*

Aimer, **adorer** and **détester** can be followed either by a noun: **J'aime le cinéma**, or by another verb. This second verb, ending in *-ing* in English, is in the infinitive in French: **J'aime lire** *I like reading*, **J'adore aller au théâtre** *I love going to the theatre*, **Je déteste regarder la télévision** *I hate watching television*.

To talk about not liking something, you put **ne** and **pas** around **aimer**: **Je n'aime pas le cinéma** *I don't like the cinema*, **Nous n'aimons pas aller au théâtre** *We don't like going to the theatre*, **Vous n'aimez pas lire?** *You don't like reading? (You can find more about negatives in the grammar section on page 135.)*

---

key vocabulary – leisure activities

regarder (un film, un DVD)	*to watch (a film, a DVD)*
écouter (la radio, de la musique)	*to listen to (the radio, music)*
lire	*to read*
rendre visite à des amis	*to visit friends*
jardiner	*to garden, do gardening*
voyager	*to travel*
faire la cuisine	*to cook*
dessiner	*to draw*
bricoler	*to do DIY*
surfer (sur internet)	*to surf (the internet)*
prendre des photos	*to take photos*
faire du shopping	*to go shopping*

have a go

footballers' lives

You come across this interview in a French magazine. It's an interview with one of Olympique de Marseille's star strikers, Claude Balabas.

▶ Read the interview and tick which of the following activities Claude enjoys.

- ❑ going to the cinema
- ❑ relaxing
- ❑ shopping
- ❑ playing golf
- ❑ cooking
- ❑ DIY

▶ Can you identify the French words or phrases for the following:

a. a star striker

b. the best football club in France

c. I like going for walks

d. I live on my own

e. a bit of everything

f. I like everything!

Claude Balabas, l'attaquant vedette du meilleur club de football de France nous parle de sa vie privée, de ce qu'il aime faire...

Claude, on vous connaît très peu finalement, au niveau personnel... Qui êtes vous? Que faites-vous dans la vie de tous les jours...?

En fait, je suis célibataire, je vis tout seul. Pendant mon temps libre, après l'entraînement, j'aime bien me reposer. De plus, c'est absolument nécessaire. Sinon, j'aime bien me promener, faire les magasins, faire la cuisine... le cinéma...

Au niveau des vêtements, la mode, c'est important pour vous?

Important? Non. Je suis quelqu'un qui aime bien les vêtements mais c'est pour me faire plaisir! J'aime également bien la musique et les voitures aussi...

La musique, c'est quoi pour vous?

Un peu de tout. Cela peut être du hip hop, du jazz, de la musique classique. J'écoute un peu de tout...

Et le cinéma?

Pareil, cela peut aller de la comédie aux films d'horreur. En fait, je ne suis pas trop difficile. J'aime tout!

Vous sortez souvent?

Pas trop. J'aime bien rester discret à la maison, avec des amis...

> making arrangements

■ ■ ■ inviting someone to do something

Tu veux venir?	*Do you want to come?*
Vous voulez venir au ciné?	*Do you want to come to the cinema?*
Tu veux faire autre chose?	*Do you want to do something else?*
On peut aller au Blues Bar, si tu veux.	*We can go to the Blues Bar, if you like.*
Et **si on faisait** un barbecue?	*Why don't we have a barbecue?*
Et **si on allait** au restaurant?	*How about going to a restaurant?*

Tu veux and **vous voulez** are present tense forms of the verb **vouloir** *to want*. The **je** form in the present is **je veux** *I want*, but in practice you're more likely to hear **Je voudrais** *I would like,* as it's more polite. Remember **vouloir** *to want* and **pouvoir** *to be able*, whose forms include **je peux** and **on peut**, are usually followed by another verb in the infinitive.

The imperfect tense is used idiomatically after **si on...** to make a suggestion.

Si on faisait un barbecue?   *Why don't we have a barbecue?*

(You can find more on the imperfect tense in the grammar section on page 132.)

se reposer	*to relax*
se promener	*to go for a walk*
le temps libre	*free time*
seul(e)	*alone*

have a go

2 social butterfly

You and your partner are on holiday in Paris where you have some friends. You call in to an internet café to check your e-mails and see that you've got three invitations for next Saturday evening. You're going to Versailles during the day on Saturday but you should be back by 7pm.

▶ Read the invitations and decide which one you will accept.

▶ Now draft an e-mail reply to one of the other two people saying you're sorry you can't come, and suggesting something else for Sunday, maybe lunch at a restaurant, or a walk, or a visit to a museum – it's your choice! Remember to say when and where to meet.

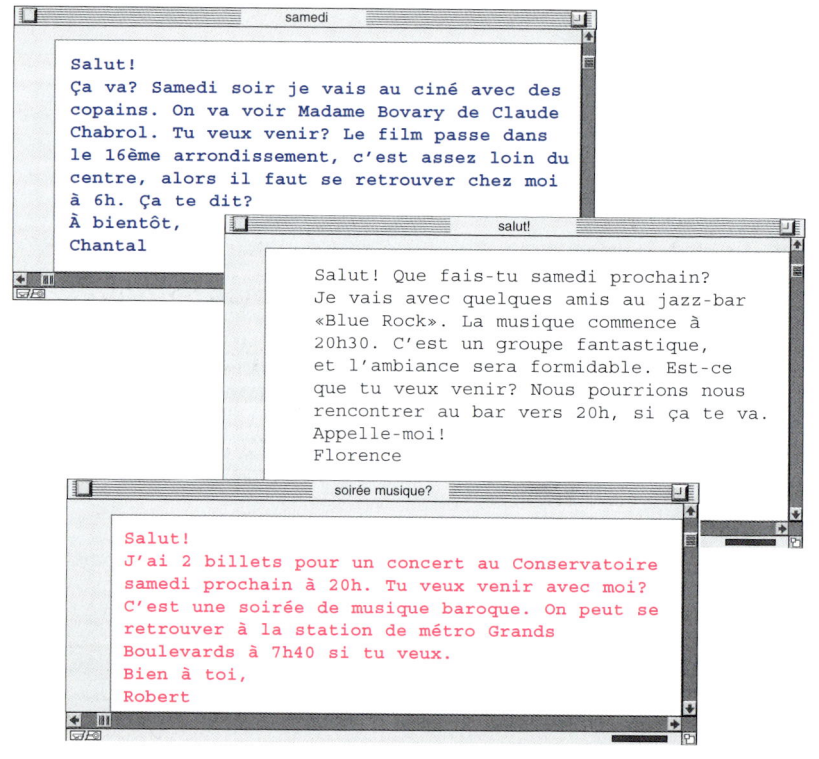

samedi

Salut!
Ça va? Samedi soir je vais au ciné avec des copains. On va voir Madame Bovary de Claude Chabrol. Tu veux venir? Le film passe dans le 16ème arrondissement, c'est assez loin du centre, alors il faut se retrouver chez moi à 6h. Ça te dit?
À bientôt,
Chantal

salut!

Salut! Que fais-tu samedi prochain?
Je vais avec quelques amis au jazz-bar «Blue Rock». La musique commence à 20h30. C'est un groupe fantastique, et l'ambiance sera formidable. Est-ce que tu veux venir? Nous pourrions nous rencontrer au bar vers 20h, si ça te va.
Appelle-moi!
Florence

soirée musique?

Salut!
J'ai 2 billets pour un concert au Conservatoire samedi prochain à 20h. Tu veux venir avec moi? C'est une soirée de musique baroque. On peut se retrouver à la station de métro Grands Boulevards à 7h40 si tu veux.
Bien à toi,
Robert

 accepting an invitation

Bar 3

D'accord!	*OK!*
Bonne idée!	*Good idea!*
Pourquoi pas?	*Why not?*
J'aimerais bien aller au ciné.	*I'd really like to go to the cinema.*
Je voudrais voir le dernier film de Luc Besson.	*I'd like to see the latest Luc Besson film.*
Je préfère aller boire un pot.	*I'd rather go for a drink.*
On se retrouve au bar à neuf heures.	*Let's meet at the bar at 9 o'clock.*
On s'appelle dimanche.	*Let's speak on the phone on Sunday.*

On literally means *one*, but in French it doesn't have the same regal connotations as in English! It's often used in the unspecific sense of *they, you, we* or just *people in general*. Verbs that follow it have the same endings as those for **il** and **elle**.

On <u>peut</u> aller au ciné.	*We can/Let's go to the cinema.*
Ici on <u>parle</u> français.	*French is spoken here.*

The **se** in **on se retrouve** and **on s'appelle** means *each other* in this context.

J'aimerais is another example of the conditional (*would*) form in French. **J'aime** *I like*; **J'aimerais** *I would like* (from **aimer** *to like*).

(For more on using the conditional tense, turn to the grammar section on page 134.)

have a go

so stylish

You find this quiz in a glossy magazine and decide to try it out.

▶ What do you discover about your style?

Petit Quiz:
Découvrez votre style

1 Quelle est votre activité préférée?
a) vous promener sur la plage
b) dîner dans un bon restaurant
c) écouter de la musique hard rock
d) faire du ski

2 Quels films préférez-vous?
a) les histoires d'amour ou de famille
b) les films policiers
c) les films d'horreur ou de sci-fi
d) les films d'action

3 Votre type d'homme ou de femme, c'est plutôt:
a) David Beckham/Britney Spears
b) George Clooney/Michelle Pfeiffer
c) Johnny Depp/Julia Roberts
d) David Ginola/Angelina Jolie

4 Votre idée d'un cadeau idéal pour une femme est:
a) des roses
b) un bijou
c) un ensemble lingerie
d) un téléphone portable

5 Choisissez une icône de mode féminine:
a) Jennifer Lopez
b) Jackie Onassis
c) Courtney Love
d) Madonna

Votre style – les résultats

Majorité de a) Votre style est romantique
Majorité de b) Votre style est classique
Majorité de c) Votre style est rock
Majorité de d) Votre style est sportif

UNIT 10

past actions, future plans

talking about the future

- discussing plans for the weekend

talking about the past

- discussing what you did at the weekend
- reporting an incident

chatting about the weather

talking about the future

discussing plans for the weekend

 Bar 3, 4

Tu as des projets pour le week-end?	*Have you got any plans for the weekend?*
On n'a rien de prévu dimanche.	*We've nothing planned on Sunday.*
On va à une exposition.	*We're going to an exhibition.*
Vendredi soir **je vais** en boîte avec des copains.	*On Friday night I'm going to a nightclub with some friends.*
Qu'est-ce que tu vas faire samedi soir?	*What are you going to do on Saturday night?*
Je vais rendre visite à un ami.	*I'm going to visit a friend.*
Je vais te donner mon numéro de portable.	*I'll give you my mobile number.*

As you can see from these examples, **on**, which literally means *one*, is often used when English uses *we*. It takes the same verb endings as **il** and **elle**: **il/elle/on va**. **On** is also used in a more undefined way to mean *people in general* or *you*:

On peut faire des sports nautiques ici?	*Can you do watersports here?*
On m'a volé mon sac!	*My bag has been stolen!*

Just as in English, if you're talking about your plans for the near future, and if the context is self-explanatory, you can use the present tense: **Vendredi je vais au ciné** *On Friday I'm going to the cinema*. You can also use the present tense of **aller** followed by another verb in the infinitive form to express that you're *going to do* something.

Je vais rendre visite à une amie samedi.	*I am going to visit a friend on Saturday.*
Je vais aller au ciné.	*I'm going to go to the cinema.*

Dimanche means *On Sunday*, whereas **le dimanche** means *on Sundays* or *every Sunday*. The same applies to the other days of the week: **Lundi on va au cinéma** *On Monday we're going to the cinema*, **Le vendredi on va à la mosquée** *On Fridays we go to the mosque*. The days of the week are not written with an initial capital letter in French.

key vocabulary – outings/meeting places

le théâtre	*theatre*
le cinéma	*cinema*
la patinoire	*skating rink*
la piscine	*swimming pool*
le parc	*park*
la boîte	*nightclub*
le match	*match*
le magasin	*shop*
le bowling	*bowling alley*
le cyber café	*internet café*

 Bar 4

Et si on faisait un barbecue?	*Why don't we have a barbecue?*
Je m'occupe des salades.	*I'll do the salads.*
Je fais un dessert et Rachid préparera le reste.	*I'll make a dessert and Rachid will prepare everything else.*

Notice how **Je m'occupe des salades** and **Je fais un dessert** both use present tense verbs but are in fact referring to the future. You can do this in informal French when you are talking about the very near future (ie within a few days) and when it is clear from the context that the future is meant – usually because a specific day is mentioned.

Using the present tense can imply certainty that something will happen, so you will often hear it after **je**. **Je fais un dessert** shows that the speaker is certain to make the dessert and **on s'appelle dimanche** implies that the speaker will definitely make a phone call. When talking about someone else's actions, the outcome is less certain, so you are more likely to hear the future tense: **Rachid préparera le reste** (equivalent to *will* in English): *Rachid will prepare everything else.*

(You can find more on talking about the future in the grammar section on page 133.)

have a go

match made in heaven?

▶ You find a fun quiz in a magazine and, out of curiosity, decide to answer it to see whether your relationship has a future.

Votre couple va-t-il durer?

Vous pensez que vous avez le parfait amour? Votre union est-elle solide comme un roc ou fragile comme du verre? Pour le savoir, faites ce test!

1 Il est de mauvaise humeur. Vous dites:
- a) Si on organisait un barbecue ou une fête pour nos amis?
- b) Si on rendait visite à ma mère?
- c) Vous ne dites rien. Vous allez sortir avec vos amies.

2 Il dit qu'il veut aller au match de foot samedi avec ses amis. Vous dites:
- a) Super idée! Moi, je vais faire du shopping. Et si on dînait en tête-à-tête samedi soir?
- b) Absolument pas. Je n'aime pas tes amis. Ils ont une mauvaise influence sur toi.
- c) Comme tu veux. Cela m'est égal – je vais aller au cinéma.

3 Dimanche vous allez faire un barbecue. Comment partagerez-vous le travail?
- a) Lui, il s'occupera des plats de viande, et vous, vous préparerez des salades.
- b) Vous préparerez tout. Lui, il ne comprend rien à la cuisine!
- c) Vous n'aurez pas le temps de l'aider. Dimanche matin vous allez faire du shopping avec une amie.

Réponses

Majorité de a) Vous avez une bonne relation. Elle va durer longtemps.
Majorité de b) Vous voulez dominer votre partenaire. L'union ne durera pas. Votre partenaire va bientôt vous quitter.
Majorité de c) Pourquoi voulez-vous être en couple? Vous serez plus heureuse seule.

partager	*to share*	vous serez	*you will be*
cela m'est égal	*I don't mind*	vous n'aurez pas	*you will not have*

❯ talking about the past

🔲🔳🔳 discussing what you did at the weekend

 Bar 5

Tu as fait du ski?	*Did you go skiing?*
J'ai fait du ski.	*I went skiing.*
On a fait de la randonnée.	*We went hiking.*
J'ai regardé la télé.	*I watched television.*
J'ai joué au tennis.	*I played tennis.*
Je n'ai pas bougé.	*I stayed in. (Literally, I didn't move.)*

J'ai fait and **on a fait** are examples of the perfect tense, which is used to talk about what has happened. In French the perfect tense has two parts: generally the present tense of **avoir** *to have* and the past participle of the main verb. It's easy to work out the past participle for the majority of verbs: for example, those ending in **-er** simply replace the **-er** with **-é**, and the pronunciation doesn't even change:

bouger →	j'ai bougé	*I moved*
payer →	j'ai payé	*I paid*
manger →	j'ai mangé	*I ate*

*(For the pattern for verbs ending in **-ir** and **-re**, see page 129.)*

Many common verbs are irregular, meaning that they are unpredictable and you need to learn their patterns separately, including their past participle. **Faire**, the past participle of which is **fait**, is one of them.

When making a verb in the perfect tense negative, put the **ne** and **pas** around the **avoir** part only:

Je n'ai pas bougé.	*I didn't move.*
Il n'a pas fait son travail.	*He didn't do his work.*

(You can find more on the perfect tense and irregular verbs in the grammar section on page 130.)

have a go

where in the world?

At your French friend's house, her little girl, who's eight years old, shows you the following quiz in her magazine. Can you help her with it?

▶ First of all, find all the words for:
   a. things to eat or drink
   b. places to visit
   c. activities to do or watch

Tu étais où?

Exemple: Tu as mangé du rosbif, tu as changé des euros en livres sterling, tu as fait une promenade en bateau sur la Tamise. Tu étais où?

Réponse: en Angleterre

Maintenant à toi.

Choisis parmi les pays suivants:

Suisse	Écosse	Russie
États-Unis	Espagne	Australie

1 Tu as mangé de la paëlla, tu as vu une course de taureaux, tu as dansé le flamenco. Tu étais où?

2 Tu as mangé du haggis, tu as parlé anglais, tu as porté un kilt. Tu étais où?

3 Tu as vu un kangourou, tu as parlé anglais, tu es allé(e) à la plage de Bondi. Tu étais où?

4 Tu as fait de l'escalade, tu as fait du ski, tu as mangé du fromage emmenthal. Tu étais où?

5 Tu as mangé des hamburgers, tu as vu un match de base-ball, tu es monté(e) à la Statue de la Liberté. Tu étais où?

6 Tu as visité le Kremlin, tes parents ont bu de la vodka, tu as acheté un samovar. Tu étais où?

Bar 5

Tu es resté(e) ici?
Je suis parti(e) à la montagne.
Je suis sorti(e) avec des copains.
On est allé(s) à la piscine.

Did you stay here?
I went off to the mountains.
I went out with some friends.
We went to the swimming pool.

A handful of verbs, including **aller**, **partir** and **rester,** form their perfect tense differently, using the present tense of **être** *to be* – **je suis, nous sommes**, etc (instead of **avoir**) before the past participle of the main verb.

With these verbs, the past participles change in spelling – you add an extra **-e**, **-s** or **-es** – depending on whether the subject is a man or woman, singular or plural. In spoken French this is irrelevant, since it doesn't affect pronunciation.

A man would write:
Je suis allé au cinéma.   *I went to the cinema.*

A woman would write:
Je suis allée au cinéma.   *I went to the cinema.*

A group of men (or men and
women) would write:
Nous sommes allés au cinéma.   *We went to the cinema.*

A group of women would write:
Nous sommes allées au cinéma.   *We went to the cinema.*

When **on** is used to mean '*we*', you may see the past participle written with an extra **-s** at the end, (or **-es** if it is an all-female group). *(You'll find a list of verbs that take **être** in the grammar section on page 130.)*

reporting an incident

On m'a volé mon sac!	*My bag has been stolen!*
Il m'a bousculé.	*He knocked into me.*
Il m'a arraché mon portable!	*He snatched my mobile phone!*
– Qu'est-ce qu'il y avait dans votre sac?	*– What did you have in your bag?*
Dans mon sac **il y avait** ma carte de crédit et mes lunettes de soleil.	*In my bag I had my credit card and my sunglasses.*
– Allez au commissariat.	*– Go to the police station.*
– Vous devez faire une déclaration.	*– You must file a report.*

Vous devez is from the verb **devoir** *to have to, must.* Another way of saying the same thing is **il faut** *(see Unit 5, page 67).*

Remember **mon**, **ma** and **mes** all mean *my*. The choice depends on what follows: **mon sac à main** (**le sac à main**) *my handbag*, **ma valise** (**la valise**) *my suitcase*, **mes vêtements** *my clothes*.

Il y avait, meaning *there was/were*, is the imperfect tense of **Il y a** *there is/there are*, another way of talking about the past. This tense is used when talking about a state or describing something in the past, rather than action. *(You'll find more on the imperfect tense in the grammar section on page 132.)*

---

key vocabulary – personal possessions

le porte-monnaie	*purse*
le portefeuille	*wallet*
la carte de crédit	*credit card*
les clés (f)	*keys*
le porte-clés	*key ring*
le passeport	*passport*
l'agenda électronique (m)	*electronic organiser*
le portable	*mobile phone*
l'appareil-photo (m)	*camera*
le caméscope	*camcorder*

have a go

daylight robbery

While waiting to report a theft in a police station, you read a notice advising victims of crime of the information the police need. You've already jotted down the time and street where the theft took place, and have prepared a summary of the incident.

▶ What haven't you yet done to complete the requirements?

**Que mettre
dans la déclaration?**

**Donnez toutes les
circonstances du sinistre:**
la nature
la date
l'heure
le lieu
les victimes

**Faites une liste des objets
volés avec leur valeur.**

have a go

4 get packing!

▶ You've booked a holiday in July in Corsica and look on a website for details about the weather. Read the summary, then say which of the following you should pack:

a. sunglasses

b. fleece

c. umbrella

d. swimming costume

e. raincoat

f. walking shoes

g. sun cream

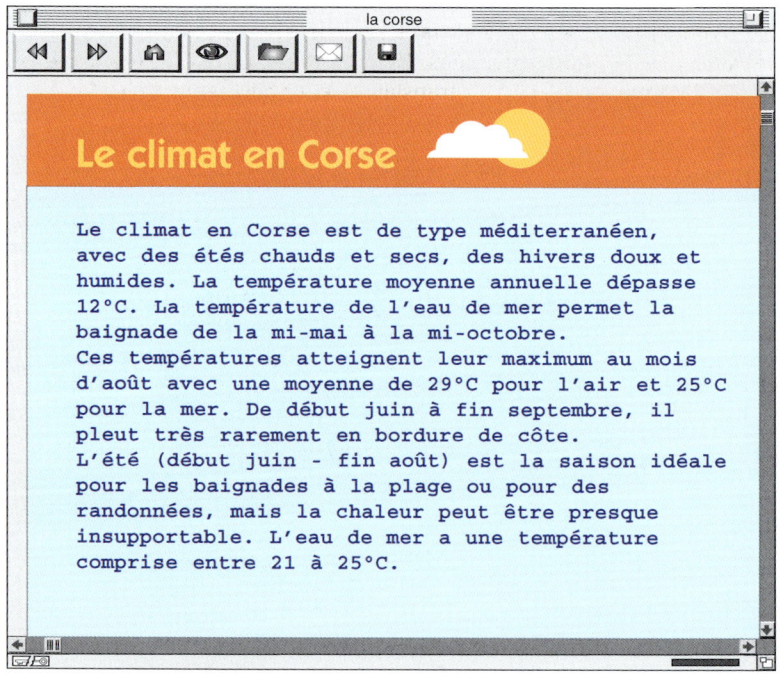

la corse

Le climat en Corse

Le climat en Corse est de type méditerranéen, avec des étés chauds et secs, des hivers doux et humides. La température moyenne annuelle dépasse 12°C. La température de l'eau de mer permet la baignade de la mi-mai à la mi-octobre.
Ces températures atteignent leur maximum au mois d'août avec une moyenne de 29°C pour l'air et 25°C pour la mer. De début juin à fin septembre, il pleut très rarement en bordure de côte.
L'été (début juin - fin août) est la saison idéale pour les baignades à la plage ou pour des randonnées, mais la chaleur peut être presque insupportable. L'eau de mer a une température comprise entre 21 à 25°C.

chatting about the weather

 Bar 4, 5; Petrol Station 4

Il fait beau.	*It's fine weather.*
Il a fait (très) beau.	*The weather was (very) fine.*
J'espère qu'**il fera** beau.	*I hope it will be fine weather.*
Il fait chaud.	*It's warm.*
Il a fait froid.	*It was cold.*
Il a fait gris.	*It was grey, dull.*
Il y a du soleil.	*It's sunny.*
Il y a des nuages.	*It's cloudy.*
Il neige.	*It's snowing.*
Il pleut.	*It's raining.*
Il a plu.	*It rained.*

As you'll have noticed, the verb **faire** is indispensable as it conveys so many different English meanings. Its basic meaning is *to do* or *make*, but when talking about weather it translates the English verb *to be*. Be sure to use the future or past of **faire** to say *it will be* fine (**il fera beau**) or *it was warm* (**il a fait chaud**).

key vocabulary – the weather

il grêle	*it's hailing*
il fait mauvais	*it's bad weather*
il fait du vent	*it's windy*
il fait du brouillard	*it's foggy*
le tonnerre	*thunder*
un orage	*a storm*
les éclairs (m)	*lightning*

have a go

5 **postcard from Paris**

You received this postcard some time ago from your Swiss friends Yvonne and Pierre.

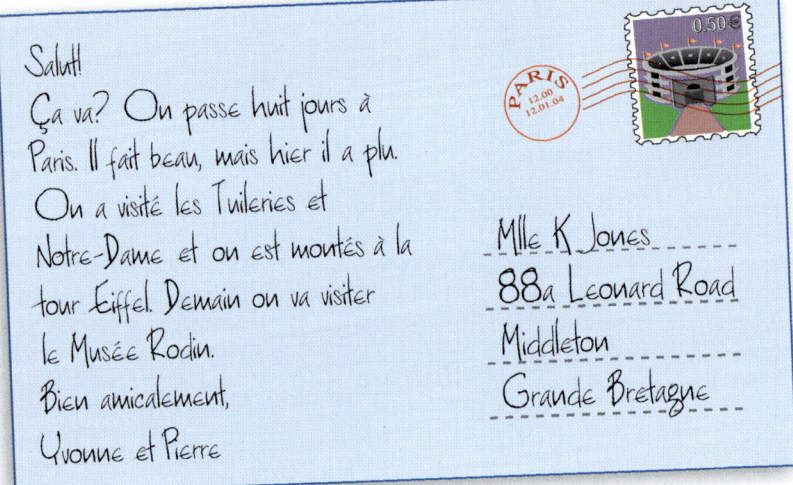

Salut!
Ça va? On passe huit jours à
Paris. Il fait beau, mais hier il a plu.
On a visité les Tuileries et
Notre-Dame et on est montés à la
tour Eiffel. Demain on va visiter
le Musée Rodin.
Bien amicalement,
Yvonne et Pierre

Mlle K Jones
88a Leonard Road
Middleton
Grande Bretagne

0.50€
PARIS
12.00
12.01.04

You're now in Paris yourself with a group of friends for a ten-day holiday. The weather is fine, but it was dull yesterday. You've been to the Louvre and Montmartre and have been up the Eiffel Tower. Tomorrow you're going to the Picasso Museum.

▶ You're about to send a few postcards to some French-speaking friends. Using Yvonne and Pierre's message as a model, highlight the words you will need to change and say what you will put instead.

grammar

CONTENTS

gender of nouns   114

plural of nouns   115

adjectives   115

possessive adjectives   117

pronouns   117

demonstratives   120

adverbs   120

quantities   121

prepositions: *à* and *de*   122

verbs in the infinitive   123

present tense   124

talking about the past   129

talking about the future   133

conditional (for polite requests)   134

imperative   135

use of *il faut*   135

negatives   135

asking questions   136

◻◼◼ gender of nouns

Nouns are words for things, people or ideas. In French, a noun is masculine or feminine. When you learn new vocabulary, learn the gender (whether it is masculine or feminine) at the same time, as it affects other words that you may want to use with the noun, such as *the*, *a* and adjectives that add descriptive detail.

Most nouns ending in a consonant are masculine, eg **le garçon**, **le chien**, **l'esprit**. Most nouns ending in an **-e** are feminine, eg **la fille**, **la bière**, **l'idée**. However, do check, because some words ending in **-e** are masculine, eg **groupe**, **monde**, **livre** (*book*). In a dictionary or wordlist the gender of each noun is indicated with *f* for feminine, *m* for masculine.

There are four words for *the*: **le** for a masculine noun, **la** for a feminine noun, **l'** instead of **le** or **la** for a noun beginning with a vowel or a silent h, **les** for a plural noun (more than one item). These words are called definite articles.

le	train (m) *the train*	les	trains *the trains*
l'	hôtel (m) *the hotel*		hôtels *the hotels*
la	chambre (f) *the room*		chambres *the rooms*
l'	école (f) *the school*		écoles *the schools*

There are two words for *a*: **un** for a masculine word, **une** for a feminine word. These are called indefinite articles.

un	train (m) *a train*	des	trains *some trains*
une	chambre (f) *a room*		chambres *some rooms*

To say *some* or *any*, use **des**, another indirect article. This must be included in French even when the words *some* or *any* can be missed out in English.

Tu as des projets pour le week-end?   *Do you have (any) plans for the weekend?*

◨◧◨ plural of nouns

Most nouns form their plural (where there is more than one) by adding an **-s**. This is only apparent in written French; it is not pronounced. French people judge whether you are talking about one thing or several by whether you say **un/le**, **une/la** or **des/les**; the noun sounds the same in both cases:

un ami	*a friend*
des amis	*some friends*
le train	*the train*
les trains	*the trains*

Nouns ending in **-eau**, like **le cadeau** *present*, **le bureau** *office*, **le morceau** *piece*, **le château** *castle* or **-eu**, like **le feu** *fire*, form their plural by adding an **-x**, still not pronounced.

un morceau de fromage	*a piece of cheese*
des morceaux de fromage	*pieces of cheese*
le feu	*the fire*
les feux	*fires, traffic lights*

Nouns ending in **-al**, like **le journal** *newspaper*, replace the **-al** with **-aux**.

un journal	*a newspaper*
des journaux	*newspapers*

If a singular noun already ends in an **-s**, the plural is the same.

mon fils	*my son*
mes fils	*my sons*

◨◧◨ adjectives

Agreement of adjectives

An adjective is used to describe a noun. In French, adjectives must 'agree' with this noun. This means that if the noun is masculine, the adjective must be in the masculine form, and if the noun is feminine, it must be in the feminine form. There are also singular and plural forms. The adjective given in the dictionary as the standard form is the masculine singular form. For the feminine singular, generally add **-e**, for the masculine plural add **-s**, and for the feminine plural **-es**.

singular	plural
un voyage intéressant (m) *an interesting journey*	**des** voyages intéressant**s** *some interesting journeys*
une histoire intéressante (f) *an interesting story*	**des** histoires intéressant**es** *some interesting stories*

Position of adjectives

Most adjectives come after the noun, as in **une banque <u>internationale</u>**. However, some frequently used adjectives go in front of the noun. For example:

le <u>premier/deuxième</u> étage	*the first/second floor*
il fait <u>beau</u> temps	*it's fine weather*
un <u>grand</u> lit et deux <u>petits</u> lits	*one big bed and two small beds*
un très <u>bon</u> restaurant	*a very good restaurant*
mon <u>nouveau</u> numéro de portable	*my new mobile number*

Some adjectives are irregular in their feminine and plural forms. Here are a few worth noting:

masculine singular	feminine singular	masculine plural	feminine plural	
rouge*	rouge	rouges	rouges	*red*
jeune*	jeune	jeunes	jeunes	*young*
bon	bonne	bons	bonnes	*good*
blanc	blanche	blancs	blanches	*white*
nouveau	nouvelle	nouveaux	nouvelles	*new*
national	nationale	nationaux	nationales	*national*
beau	belle	beaux	belles	*beautiful, fine*

*if the masculine form ends in **-e**, don't add another in the feminine form.

une banque <u>nationale</u>	*a national bank*
l'entrecôte est très <u>bonne</u>	*the steak is excellent*
un kilo de pêches <u>blanches</u>	*a kilo of white peaches*

🟨🟥🟧 possessive adjectives

In French, the words for *my*, *your*, *his*, *her*, *our* and *their* agree in gender and number with the noun they refer to. The gender of the speaker is irrelevant; it is the following noun that determines which form of the word to use.

le	sac *the bag*	mon	sac *my bags*
l'	appartement (m) *the apartment* école (f) *the school*	mon	appartement *my apartment* école *my school*
la	valise *the suitcase*	ma	valise *my suitcase*
les	sacs *the bags* valises *the suitcases*	mes	sacs *my bags* valises *my suitcases*

The same pattern followed by **mon, ma, mes** also applies to **ton, ta, tes** (*your*) and for **son, sa, ses** (*his/her*). They always agree with the person or thing possessed. The words for *our:* **notre**, **nos**, and *your:* **votre**, **vos**, don't change whether the noun is masculine or feminine.

votre carte de crédit (la carte de crédit)   *your credit card*
à votre service (le service)   *at your service*

🟨🟥🟧 pronouns

Subject pronouns

Je, **tu**, **il**, **elle**, **on**, **nous**, **vous**, **ils** and **elles** are subject pronouns, so called because they act as the subject of the verb.

Je prends le plat du jour.   *I'll have the dish of the day.*
Tu veux venir?   *Do you want to come?*
Il fait beau.   *It's fine weather.*

Je means *I*. It is written with a lower-case letter j if it doesn't start a sentence. It is shortened to **j'** before a vowel or a silent h: **j'aime la France** *I like France*, **j'habite à Paris** *I live in Paris*.

Tu and **vous** both mean *you*. **Tu** is used to talk to one person, who is a friend, a relative or a young person. **Vous** is used to talk to one person in a formal way, or to more than one person. It is used in shops, restaurants, to strangers in the street and in other formal situations. **Nous** means *we*.

Il and **elle** mean *he* and *she* (or *it*), while **ils** and **elles** mean *they*. These pronouns agree with the gender of the noun they replace.

On is a subject pronoun that is used a lot in spoken French. It literally means *one* but is often used where in English we would say *we* or *you*. It is followed by the same verb endings as **il** and **elle**.

<u>On</u> peut aller au musée.
We can go/Let's go to the museum.

Qu'est-ce qu'<u>on</u> peut faire comme activités?
What sort of activities can you do?

subject *(I, you, etc)*	direct object *(me, you, etc)*	indirect object *(to me, to you, etc)*	reflexive *(myself, yourself, etc)*
je	me	me	me
tu	te	te	te
elle	la	lui	se
il	le	lui	se
on	le	lui	se
nous	nous	nous	nous
vous	vous	vous	vous
elles	les	leur	se
ils	les	leur	se

Object pronouns

Object pronouns are all the words used for *me, you, him, her, it, us, them*. In the sentence *I love him*, the word *I* acts as the subject of the verb, the one carrying out the action; *him* is the object of the verb, the one affected by it. In the sentence *He loves me, he* is the subject and the word *me* is the object of the verb.

Direct object pronouns

There are direct object pronouns, used when the noun is acted on directly: **Anne les regarde** *Anne is watching them*. There are indirect object pronouns, used to say to *me, to her, to them* and so on: **Anne leur parle** *Anne is talking to them*.

In an English sentence, the usual word order is:

▸ **subject – verb – object** (or **object pronoun**).

In French the object pronoun usually comes before the relevant verb.

Vous l'avez en noir en 40?	*Do you have it in black in a size 40?*
(**l'** is short for '**le**' referring to '**le** chemisier')	
Je la prends	*I'll take it.*
('**la**' refers to '**la** chambre')	
Vous les prenez?	*Are you taking them?*
('**les**' refers to '**les** bottines')	

Indirect object pronouns

The pronouns **le**, **la**, **l'**, **les** mean *him/it, her/it* and *them*. If you want to say *to him, to her* or *to them*, you need to use **lui** and **leur** even if the word '*to*' is only understood, not explicitly stated, as in *Can you tell (say to) him?* Use **lui** for *to him* or *to her* and **leur** for *to them*.

*Vous pouvez **lui** dire...?	*Can you tell (to) him...?*
Je leur conseille les films	*I recommend (to them) the films*
de Jean-Luc Godard.	*of Jean-Luc Godard.*

Me, **te**, **vous** and **nous** mean *to me/to you/to us* as well as simply *me/you/us*.

*Vous pouvez **me** recommander	*Can you recommend (to me) a*
un restaurant?	*restaurant?*
Je vous conseille cette crème.	*I recommend (to you) this cream.*

*When there are two verbs together, the pronoun comes just before the verb it refers to, ie the infinitive.

🟨🟥🟧 demonstratives

Demonstratives are words like *this* and *that*, or *this one*, used to indicate particular items. The French words for *this, that, these, those* (demonstrative adjectives) are shown below:

	singular	plural
le vase *the vase* l'hôtel *the hotel*	**ce** vase *this/that vase* **cet** hôtel *this/that hotel*	**ces** vases *these/those vases* **ces** hôtels *these/those hotels*
la carte *the card*	**cette** carte *this/that card*	**ces** cartes *these/those cards*

To emphasise *this* or *that*, simply tag **-ci** or **-là** to the end of the noun.

Je voudrais ce vase-<u>là</u>.	*I'd like that vase.*
Je préfère ce vase-<u>ci</u>.	*I prefer this vase.*

If you want to say *this one* or *that one* without naming the actual noun, use the pronouns **celui-ci** or **celui-là** for masculine words, and **celle-ci** and **celle-là** for feminine nouns:

Je voudrais celui-ci.	*I'd like this one. (refers to* **le vase**, *or any masculine noun)*
Je voudrais celui-là.	*I'd like that one. (refers to* **le vase**, *or any masculine noun)*
Je prends celle-ci.	*I'll take this one. (refers to* **la carte**, *or any feminine noun)*
Je prends celle-là.	*I'll take that one. (refers to* **la carte**, *or any feminine noun)*

🟨🟥🟧 adverbs

Adverbs describe or modify the meaning of other words in the sentence – often a verb or an adjective. Adverbs give more information about how, where or when something is done. The endings of adverbs never change. Just as many English adverbs end in *-ly*, many French adverbs end in **-ment**.

C'est où <u>exactement</u>?	*Where is it <u>exactly</u>?*
Je suis <u>vraiment</u> désolé(e).	*I'm <u>really</u> sorry.*
Je n'ai pas de monnaie, <u>seulement</u> un billet de 50€.	*I haven't any change, <u>only</u> a 50€ note.*

However, there are some adverbs that don't fit the pattern. A few useful ones are:

tout de suite	*immediately*
souvent	*often*
plutôt	*rather*
encore	*still, again*
bien, mieux	*well, better*
bientôt	*soon*
vite	*quickly*

 quantities

To express 'some' or 'any'

Use **du** for masculine words, **de la** for feminine, **de l'** for words of either gender that begin with a vowel or silent h, and **des** for plural.

le fromage	**du** fromage *(some cheese)*
la viande	**de** la viande *(some meat)*
l'eau minérale	**de** l'eau minérale *(some mineral water)*
les glaces	**des** glaces *(some ice creams)*

Je voudrais du jambon.	*I'd like some ham.*
Est-ce qu'il y a de la viande dans le gratin?	*Is there (any) meat in the gratin?*

After a negative, always use **de** or **d'**, whether the noun is singular or plural.

Il n'y a pas de télécommande.	*There is no remote control.*
Je n'ai pas de monnaie.	*I haven't got any change.*
Nous n'avons pas de chambres.	*We haven't got any rooms.*

To express 'of' with specific measures

If you specify an amount or quantity, *of* is always translated by **de**, regardless of the gender or number of the noun. **De** becomes **d'** before a vowel or silent h.

une carafe d'eau minérale	*a carafe of mineral water*
une bouteille de vin rouge	*a bottle of red wine*
un kilo/300 grammes/une livre de pêches/tomates	*a kilo/300gm/a pound of peaches/tomatoes*
un morceau/dix tranches de saucisson	*a piece/ten slices of sausage*
une boîte de thon	*a tin of tuna*
Il y a beaucoup de circulation.	*There's a lot of traffic.*
J'ai un peu de vin.	*I've got a little wine.*

🟨🟥🟧 prepositions: *à* and *de*

à

The preposition **à** is used:

– with names of places and locations, meaning *to*, *at* or *in*:

eg Je travaille à Nanterre.	*I work in Nanterre.*
Je vais à l'hôtel.	*I am going to the hotel.*
... à la gare	*... to the station*
... au restaurant	*... to the restaurant*
... aux magasins	*... to the shops*
Il est à la réception.	*He is at reception.*

– with numbers and prices:

eg Deux menus à quinze euros.	*Two fifteen-euro menus.*

– to specify distance:

eg C'est à 15 kilomètres d'ici.	*It's fifteen kilometres from here.*
C'est à dix minutes à pied.	*It's ten minutes' walk away.*

– in the expression **avoir mal à**:

eg J'ai mal à la tête.	*I have a headache.*
J'ai mal au pied.	*I have a sore foot.*
J'ai mal aux dents.	*I have toothache.*

– to specify flavours:

eg des glaces à la fraise/au chocolat	*strawberry/chocolate ice-creams*
une tarte aux fruits	*a fruit tart*

As you can see from these examples, **à** cannot be followed by **le** or **les**; it changes to **au** or **aux** respectively.

de

The preposition **de** is used:

– to talk about possession or belonging, similar to the usage of 's in English:

la sœur de Marianne	*Marianne's sister*
	(= the sister of Marianne)
le chien des voisins	*the neighbours' dog*
	(= the dog of the neighbours)

– to specify where someone or something is from:

Je suis de Nice.	*I'm from Nice.*
le train de Paris	*the train from Paris*
Je viens de France/du Maroc.	*I come from France/Morocco.*

Note that **de** needs the article with masculine singular and masculine plural countries, eg **Je suis du** (=de+le) **Brésil** and **Je suis des** (=de+les) **États-Unis**, but not for feminine countries (eg **Je suis de France**).

– in negative sentences (see page 121 for the use of *some* and *any* in sentences that aren't negative):

Je n'ai pas de monnaie.	*I haven't got any change.*
Je n'ai plus de glaces à l'abricot.	*I haven't got any more apricot ice-creams.*

Remember, **de** cannot be followed by **le** or **les** – it becomes **du** or **des** respectively.

🟨🟧🟥 verbs in the infinitive

The basic form of the verb – the part you'll find in a dictionary – is called the infinitive. English infinitives begin with the word *to*. Most French infintives end with the letters **-er**, **-ir**, or **-re**. For example:

travailler	*to work*
finir	*to finish*
attendre	*to wait*
faire	*to do*
avoir	*to have*

Many verbs follow a regular pattern. Those that don't are called irregular verbs.

🟨🟧🟥 present tense

Whereas in English there are two ways to express the present tense (*I work* or *I am working*) there is only one form in French (**je travaille**).

Regular verbs belong to one of three groups:

1 Verbs whose infinitives end in **-er**, such as **travailler** *to work*, **donner** *to give*, **aimer** *to love*.

To form the present tense, take off the **-er**. The part of the verb you are left with is called the stem. With regular **-er** verbs such as **travailler**, add the following endings to the stem:

travailler *to work*

je travaille	*I work*	nous travaillons	*we work*
tu travailles	*you work*	vous travaillez	*you work*
il/elle/on travaille	*he/she/it works*	ils/elles travaillent	*they work*

Je travaille à Nanterre.   *I work in Nanterre.*
Vous acceptez la carte Visa?   *Do you accept Visa?*
Je cherche le rayon des jouets.   *I am looking for the toy department.*

2 Verbs whose infinitives end in **-ir**, such as **finir** *to finish*, **choisir** *to choose*.

To form the present tense of regular **-ir** verbs, take off the **-ir** and add the following endings:

finir *to finish*

je finis	*I finish*	nous finissons	*we finish*
tu finis	*you finish*	vous finissez	*you finish*
il/elle/on finit	*he/she/it finishes*	ils/elles finissent	*they finish*

Vous finissez le travail à quelle heure? *What time do you finish work?*

3 Verbs whose infinitives end in **-re**, such as **attendre** *to wait*, **rendre** *to give back*, **descendre** *to get down/off*.

To form the present tense of regular **-re** verbs, take off the **-re** and add the following endings:

---

attendre *to wait*

j'attends	*I wait*	nous attendons	*we wait*
tu attends	*you wait*	vous attendez	*you wait*
il/elle/on attend	*he/she/it waits*	ils/elles attendent	*they wait*

Je descends où? *Where do I get off?*

Irregular verbs

Many common verbs are irregular and do not follow these patterns, although you will notice similarities.

Note also that you cannot always translate literally from English to French. In English we say *he is ten years old*, using the verb *to be* (which is **être** in French), whereas in French you say **il a dix ans** (from the verb **avoir**), *he has ten years*. When talking about the weather we say in English *it is fine* etc, whereas in French the verb **faire** (literally *to do, make*) is used: **Il fait gris** *It's dull*.

The verbs **avoir** and **être** are called auxiliary verbs. They can be used on their own or as part of the perfect tense. (See page 129.)

être *to be*

je suis	*I am*	nous sommes	*we are*
tu es	*you are*	vous êtes	*you are*
il/elle/on est	*he/she/it is*	ils/elles sont	*they are*

Vous êtes sûr(e)?	*Are you sure?*
Je suis de Paris.	*I am from Paris.*
Quelle heure est-il?	*What time is it?*
Il est cinq heures.	*It's 5 o'clock.*

avoir *to have*

j'ai	*I have*	nous avons	*we have*
tu as	*you have*	vous avez	*you have*
il/elle/on a	*he/she/it has*	ils/elles ont	*they have*

Qu'est-ce que vous avez?	*What do you have?*
Quel âge avez-vous?	*How old are you?*
J'ai vingt ans.	*I'm 20.*

Here are some more common irregular verbs:

aller *to go*

je vais	*I go*	nous allons	*we go*
tu vas	*you go*	vous allez	*you go*
il/elle/on va	*he/she/it goes*	ils/elles vont	*they go*

Je vais en boîte.	*I'm going to a nightclub.*
Ça va?	*Is that OK?/How are you?*

boire *to drink*

je bois	*I drink*	nous buvons	*we drink*
tu bois	*you drink*	vous buvez	*you drink*
il/elle/on boit	*he/she/it drinks*	ils/elles boivent	*they drink*

Qu'est-ce que vous buvez?	*What are you drinking?*

dire *to say*

je dis	*I say*	nous disons	*we say*
tu dis	*you say*	vous dites	*you say*
il/elle/on dit	*he/she/it says*	ils/elles disent	*they say*

Dites-moi.	*Tell me.*

faire *to do, make*

je fais	I do	nous faisons	we do
tu fais	you do	vous faites	you do
il/elle/on fait	he/she/it does	ils/elles font	they do

Je fais un dessert.	I'm making a dessert.
Il fait beau aujourd'hui.	It's fine today.
Ça fait combien?	How much is it?
Je fais du 38.	I'm a size 38.

prendre *to take*

je prends	I take	nous prenons	we take
tu prends	you take	vous prenez	you take
il/elle/on prend	he/she/it takes	ils/elles prennent	they take

| Je prends le plat du jour. | I'll have the dish of the day. |
| Vous prenez un dessert? | Are you having (literally *taking*) a dessert? |

savoir *to know (how to)*

je sais	I know	nous savons	we know
tu sais	you know	vous savez	you know
il/elle/on sait	he/she/it knows	ils/elles savent	they know

Vous savez où sont les toilettes?	Do you know where the toilets are?
Oui, je sais.	Yes, I know.
Il ne sait pas nager.	He doesn't know how to swim.

venir *to come*

je viens	I come	nous venons	we come
tu viens	you come	vous venez	you come
il/elle/on vient	he/she/it comes	ils/elles viennent	they come

| Vous venez d'où? | Where do you come from? |

The next three irregular verbs, **pouvoir** *to be able*, **vouloir** *to want*, and **devoir** *to have to, must*, are called modal verbs. They are the verbs needed for saying what you *should, must, can, ought* or *want* to do, and are often followed by another verb in the infinitive form.

pouvoir *to be able to, can*

je peux	I can	nous pouvons	we can
tu peux	you can	vous pouvez	you can
il/elle/on peut	he/she/it can	ils/elles peuvent	they can

Je peux avoir un reçu?   *Can I have a receipt?*
On peut aller au Blues Bar.   *We can go to the Blues Bar.*

vouloir *to want*

je veux	I want	nous voulons	we want
tu veux	you want	vous voulez	you want
il/elle/on veut	he/she/it wants	ils/elles veulent	they want

Tu veux venir?   *Do you want to come?*

devoir *to have to, must; to owe*

je dois	I must	nous devons	we must
tu dois	you must	vous devez	you must
il/elle/on doit	he/she/it must	ils/elles doivent	they must

Vous devez faire une déclaration.   *You must file a report.*
Je vous dois combien?   *How much do I owe you?*

◼◼◼ talking about the past

1 Perfect tense

This tense is used to talk about something you did or have done, or something that happened in the past. It is by far the most commonly used past tense in French. It's made up of two parts: in most cases these are the present tense of **avoir** and the past participle of the verb, which doesn't change. (*See page 126 for the present tense of* **avoir**.)

To form the past participle of regular verbs whose infinitive ends in **-er**, replace **-er** with **-é**:

réservé (from **réserver**)	**J'ai réservé une chambre.**	*I've reserved a room.*
volé (from **voler**)	**Il a volé mon sac.**	*He stole my bag.*
terminé (from **terminer**)	**Vous avez terminé?**	*Have you finished?*

The past participle of regular **-ir** verbs ends in **-i** and of regular **-re** verbs in **-u**.

fini (from **finir**)	**Vous avez fini?**	*Have you finished?*
attendu (from **attendre**)	**J'ai attendu cinq minutes.**	*I waited five minutes.*

Some verbs are irregular and you just have to learn their past participle. However, once learnt, it never changes!

Il a <u>fait</u> beau. (from **faire**)	*It was fine.*
Il a <u>plu</u>. (from **pleuvoir**)	*It rained.*
Nous avons <u>pris</u> deux menus à 15 euros. (from **prendre**)	*We had two 15-euro menus.*

A number of useful verbs form their perfect tense using the present tense of **être**, not **avoir**. (*See page 125 for the present tense of* **être**.) These are usually verbs indicating movement or a change of state:

infinitive		past participle
aller	*to go*	allé
venir	*to come*	venu
arriver	*to arrive*	arrivé
partir	*to leave*	parti
entrer	*to enter*	entré
sortir	*to go out*	sorti
monter	*to climb*	monté
descendre	*to go down*	descendu
revenir	*to come back*	revenu
rentrer	*to go/come back in*	rentré
retourner	*to return*	retourné
tomber	*to fall*	tombé
rester	*to stay*	resté
naître	*to be born*	né
mourir	*to die*	mort

Vous êtes arrivé aujourd'hui?	*Did you arrive today?*
Je suis parti à la montagne.	*I went to the mountains.*
Tu es resté ici?	*Did you stay here?*

For **être** verbs, the past participle changes its ending depending on the gender and number of the subject. This means that you have to take into account who is doing the coming, going, etc. Is it one man, one woman, or more than one?

Feminine singular (**je**, **tu**, **elle**, **vous**): add **-e**

Je suis arrivée aujourd'hui.	*I arrived today.* (woman speaking)
Tu es allée où le week-end dernier?	*Where did you go last weekend?* (said to a girl or woman)
Sophie est rentrée à la maison à neuf heures.	*Sophie came home at 9 o'clock.* (refers to a woman)

Masculine plural, or mixed groups (**nous**, **vous**, **ils**): add **-s**

Ils sont allés au cinéma vendredi soir.	*They went to the cinema on Friday evening.* (refers to men or to a mixed group)
Nous sommes rentrés des États-Unis lundi.	*We came back from the States on Monday.* (refers to men or to a mixed group)
Vous êtes allés à la plage aujourd'hui?	*Did you go to the beach today?* (spoken to a group of men or a mixed group)

Feminine plural (**nous**, **vous**, **elles**): add **-es**

Nathalie et Sylvie sont allées au cinéma.	*Natalie and Silvie went to the cinema.*
Nous sommes rentrées de Nantes à dix-huit heures.	*We returned from Nantes at 6pm.* (both refer to women only)

Any group referred to using **on** when it means *we*: can add **-s**, although both spellings are acceptable.

In this case, the past participle can be treated as plural, even though **on** is a singular pronoun and takes the same form of the verb as **il** and **elle**.

On est allé(s) au cinéma.	*We went to the cinema.*

Note that the pronunciation of the past participle doesn't change, whether it's masculine, feminine or plural.

2 Imperfect tense

This is used to describe people, things and places in the past. It's also used to talk about past actions that were habitual or continuous.

To form the imperfect tense, take the **nous** part of the present tense, eg **nous avons** (*we have*) or **nous faisons** (*we make*), take off the **-ons**, and replace it with the following endings:

j'av<u>ais</u>	*I had*
tu av<u>ais</u>	*you had*
il/elle/on av<u>ait</u>	*he/she/it had*
nous av<u>ions</u>	*we had*
vous av<u>iez</u>	*you had*
ils/elles av<u>aient</u>	*they had*

There is only one exception to this and that is **être**, whose imperfect tense endings are added to the stem **ét-**, for example **j'étais, tu étais**.

C'était délicieux.	*It was delicious.*
L'entrecôte était vraiment excellente.	*The steak was really excellent.*

The imperfect tense is also used idiomatically after **Si on...** to make a suggestion. For example:

Si on faisait un barbecue?	*Why don't we have a barbecue?*

3 Using depuis

To describe an action that started in the past and is still going on now, use **depuis** with the present tense.

J'habite à Paris depuis cinq ans.	*I have been in Paris for five years (and still live here).*
Je travaille à Nanterre depuis novembre dernier.	*I've been working in Nanterre since last November.*
J'ai mal à la tête depuis deux jours.	*I've had a headache for two days.*

You only use **depuis** if the action is still going on now. If the action was in the past, use the perfect tense and **pendant** to mean *for*.

J'ai habité à Paris pendant deux ans.	*I lived in Paris for two years (but don't live there now).*

4 Using venir de

To say you have just done something in the very recent past, use the present tense of **venir** followed by **de** followed by an infinitive.

Je <u>viens de</u> tomber en panne.   *I have just broken down.*
Vous <u>venez d'</u>arriver?   *Have you just arrived?*
Le train <u>vient de</u> partir.   *The train has just left.*
Un jeune homme <u>vient de</u> voler   *A young man has just stolen my*
  mon sac.   *bag.*

talking about the future

1 Using the present tense

If you're talking about your plans for the very near future (often a specific day or time is mentioned), use the present tense. Using the present tense implies certainty that you *will* do something.

Vendredi, je vais au ciné.   *On Friday I'm going to the cinema.*
Ce soir je fais un dessert.   *Tonight, I'll make a dessert.*

2 Using aller + infinitive

Just as in English when you say you are *going to do* something, in French you can use the present tense of **aller** *to go* followed by another verb in the infinitive form.

Je vais aller au ciné.   *I am going to go to the cinema.*
Je vais rendre visite à une amie   *I am going to visit a friend on*
  samedi.   *Saturday.*
Ça va me prendre longtemps?   *Is it going to take me long?*

3 Using the future tense

Otherwise, French has a future tense to talk about the future. For most verbs this is formed by adding the endings **-ai**, **-as**, **-a**, **-ons**, **-ez** and **-ont** to the infinitive. If the infinitive ends in an **-e**, knock this off first. This means that there is always a letter **r** before the ending.

> **préparer** *to prepare*
>
> | | | | |
> |---|---|---|---|
> | je prépare**rai** | *I will prepare* | nous prépare**rons** | *we will prepare* |
> | tu prépare**ras** | *you will prepare* | vous prépare**rez** | *you will prepare* |
> | il/elle/on prépare**ra** | *he/she/it will prepare* | ils/elles prépare**ront** | *they will prepare* |

There are the usual irregular verbs that do not obey this rule. For these, use the same endings, but tag them on to a special stem, not the infinitive.

être uses the stem **ser-**	je serai, etc.
avoir uses the stem **aur-**	j'aurai, etc.
faire uses the stem **fer-**	je ferai, etc.
aller uses the stem **ir-**	j'irai, etc.
pouvoir uses the stem **pourr-**	je pourrai, etc.
vouloir uses the stem **voudr-**	je voudrai, etc.

Rachid préparera une salade.	*Rachid will prepare a salad.*
J'espère qu'il fera beau.	*I hope the weather will be nice.*

▢▣▣ conditional (for polite requests)

Use the conditional rather than the present tense when you are making a polite request or are asking rather tentatively.

The conditional endings are the same as those of the imperfect tense: **-ais, -ais, -ait, -ions, -iez, -aient.** These are added to the stem used in the future tense, which always ends in **-r**.

Je veux...	*I want...*
Je <u>voudrais</u>...	*I would like...*
J'aime...	*I like...*
J'<u>aimerais</u>...	*I would like...*
Je peux avoir...?	*Can I have...?*
Je <u>pourrais</u> avoir...?	*Could I have...?*

▣▣▣ imperative

To give a command, instruction or advice, use the imperative. The imperative is formed using the **vous** or **tu** part of the present tense, but without saying the word **vous** or **tu**.

tu form	*Traverse la rue.	Prends ces comprimés.	Viens avec moi.
vous form	Traversez la rue.	Prenez ces comprimés.	Venez avec moi.
	Cross the road.	*Take these tablets.*	*Come with me.*

* Note that the **tu** form of **-er** verbs drops the **-s**.

▣▣▣ use of *il faut*

Il faut expresses need or obligation. It can be translated as *I/you must, I/you have to, I/you/we need to, it is necessary to.* The context will make it clear whether you mean *you, I* or *we*. **Il faut** is often followed by another verb in the infinitive:

Il faut aller chez le médecin.	*You must go to the doctor's.*
Il faut venir au bureau.	*You need to come to the office.*
Il faut prendre quelle ligne?	*Which line do I have to take?*

▣▣▣ negatives

To make a verb negative, put **ne ... pas** around it.

Le téléphone ne marche pas.	*The telephone isn't working.*
La voiture ne démarre pas.	*The car won't start.*
Je n'aime pas danser.	*I don't like dancing.*
Ce n'est pas grave.	*It's not serious.*

However, in spoken French the **ne** is often dropped. So you will often hear **C'est pas grave** for example.

If there are any pronouns before the verb, the **ne** comes before them:

Il n'y a pas beaucoup de circulation.	*There isn't much traffic.*
Les films de Jacques Tati, je ne les aime pas.	*I don't like the films of Jacques Tati.*

In the perfect tense, the **ne ... pas** goes around the **avoir** or **être** part only.

Je n'ai pas bougé.   *I didn't move.*

Pas can also be replaced by other negative words:

ne ... rien	*nothing*
ne ... plus	*no longer, no more*
ne ... jamais	*never*

Je ne peux rien faire pour vous ici.   *I can't do anything for you here.*
Je n'ai plus de glaces au chocolat.   *I've no more chocolate ice-creams.*

🟡🟥🟥 asking questions

The easiest way to ask a question is to raise your voice at the end of the sentence:

On peut dîner à l'hôtel?   *Is it possible to have dinner in the hotel?*

Il y a un bar?   *Is there a bar?*

Without the question mark and the rising intonation, these are simple statements: *It is possible to have dinner at the hotel* and *There is a bar.*

Alternatively, to ensure that people realise you are asking a question, you can start with **Est-ce que** and then say your sentence with rising intonation. This phrase means approximately *Is it that....?* and converts a statement into a question.

Est-ce qu'on peut dîner à l'hôtel?   *Is it possible to have dinner at the hotel?*

Est-ce qu'il y a un bar?   *Is there a bar?*

Question words

You can ask a question by using one of the following question words:

où...?	*where...?*
qui...?	*who, whom...?*
quand...?	*when...?*
combien (de...)?	*how many...? how much...?*
comment...?	*how...?*

pourquoi...?	*why...?*
quoi...?	*what...?*
que/qu'est-ce que...?	*what...?*
quel(le)...?	*what...? which...?*

These can be used on their own, eg **Pourquoi?** *Why?* They often appear at the end of a question:

Vous venez d'où?	*Where do you come from?*
Tu as invité qui?	*Who have you invited?*
Ils arrivent quand?	*When are they arriving?*
Il s'appelle comment?	*What's his name?*

If they appear at the start of a question, then the subject and verb swap places, ie the verb comes first:

Où se trouve le musée exactement?	*Where exactly is the museum?*
Où sont les ascenseurs?	*Where are the lifts?*

Or you can add **est-ce que** just after the question word:

Où est-ce que vous travaillez?	*Where do you work?*
Qu'est-ce que vous faites?	*What do you do?/What are you doing?*

French often forms questions with **c'est** at the beginning, plus a question word:

C'est quoi le poulet basquaise?	*What is chicken Basquaise?*
C'est combien cette chemise?	*How much is this shirt?*
C'est à quelle heure le petit déjeuner?	*What time is breakfast?*

Quel is an adjective, so it has feminine and plural endings (**quelle, quels, quelles**) and there is always an accompanying noun in the sentence (although it's not necessarily the next word – it may be separated by **être**):

Quel est le plat du jour?	*What's the dish of the day?*
Le petit déjeuner est à quelle heure?	*What time is breakfast?*
Quels sports nautiques est-ce qu'on peut faire?	*What watersports can we do?*
Tu préfères quelles chaussures?	*Which shoes do you prefer?*

answers

See below for all the answers to the **have a go** sections:

unit 1

1 soap box, page 23
Julien is the daughter's fiancé, news that came as a surprise to her mother. He's from Senegal but has been living in Meaux for five years. Rachid is Didier's colleague from the merchant bank. He's a programmer-analyst.

2 chit chat, page 26
Bonjour à tous! Je suis étudiante, 22 ans, célibataire, jolie blonde. Je recherche des correspondants en France. J'attends une réponse avec impatience.

unit 2

1 feeling peckish, page 30
You – sandwich au fromage, chocolat chaud; Isobel – sandwich au jambon, bière; Meera – omelette, eau minérale.

2 culinary quiz, page 33
Ratatouille – B; salade niçoise – C; cassoulet – A

There are seven vegetables (or eight if you count tomates – tomatoes!): haricots – beans; poivrons – peppers; courgettes – courgettes; aubergines – aubergines; oignons – onions; concombre – cucumber; fèves – broad beans.

3 rave reviews, page 35
Un bon resto. Le service est très bon et les plats excellents. Le patron est très sympa.

4 final reckoning, page 37
There is a mistake in the bill: it states that you had an apricot flan (flan aux abricots) instead of a fruit salad (salade de fruits). Service is included.

unit 3

1 mountain adventure, page 40
Monsieur,
Je voudrais savoir si vous avez *trois* chambres libres du *2 au 9 novembre*. Je cherche une chambre pour trois personnes (un adulte et deux enfants) et *deux chambres* pour une personne.
Sincères salutations.

2 speed dial, page 42
a) 225 b) 125 c) 220 d) 9 e) 125

f) You don't need to dial a number, you can make yourself a cup of tea as there's a courtesy tray in the room; g) ring 195 for the Restaurant Océane; h) Ring 240 for room service; i) ring 170 for the Restaurant Panoramique.

3 hotel horror, page 44
(In order) climatiseur, machine à café, savon.

4 happy families, page 47
You should investigate la chambre d'hôte and l'auberge de pays.

The words are:
charme – charm; convivialité – conviviality; découvrir – discover; apprécier – appreciate; différentes –

different; spécialitiés – specialities; locales – local; régionale – regional; rural – rural; indépendant – independent; situé – situated; ferme – farm; village – village; week-end – weekend; propriétaire – proprietor; offre – to offer; traditionnelle – traditional; confort – comfort; parfaite – perfect; simplicité – simplicity.

unit 4

1 going underground, page 51
a) You can buy a single ticket for $2.50 or you can buy a book of six tickets for $11. You can also buy a tourist ticket, which gives you unlimited travel for one day for $8, or for three days for $16.
b) No, the last train leaves at 12.30pm on weekdays and Sundays, and at 1am on Saturdays.
c) You have to scratch the relevant day or days and month on the ticket.

2 signs of the times, page 54
No, vehicles come out through the gate.

Give way to traffic from the right.

3 roadside rescue, page 55
Yes; 'recherche véhicule' means they'll come out and get your vehicle.

Le plein de sans plomb, s'il vous plaît! – Fill her up with unleaded, please! Pouvez vous vérifier la pression des pneus? – Could you check the tyre pressure?

4 taxi tales, page 57
a) 90 euros.
b) Probably, but you need to contact them.
c) Luggage taken free of charge.

unit 5

1 streets ahead, page 61
The Chinese restaurant (le Resto Mingo Ho) is number 2; number 1 is the post office (la poste) and number 7 is the museum (le musée), and the unidentified square is number 8.

2 way to go, page 65
Look for a 15-storey glass building, then cross the little bridge opposite it, on your right. Next, turn left and look out for some traffic lights. Your friend's office is next to the Café Picasso, on the right.

3 route to victory, page 66
Coming from the A55, at the end of the motorway, take the tunnel sign-posted 'centre-ville'. Follow the promenade Pompidou until the war memorial. Take the avenue du Palais as far as the roundabout, then take the southern exit (boulevard Victor Hugo). Continue until the obelisk. Once on the roundabout, turn left on to avenue du Maréchal Lyautey and continue until you reach Saint Martin's church. Take the right and follow the road as far as the stadium.

There are two roundabouts.

unit 6

1 cartoon culture, page 71
The Clockarium, open both days; the Musée d'Art Fantastique, open both days but only in the afternoons; the Centre Belge de la Bande Dessinée, open both days. (The Musée de l'Eau et de la Fontaine is only open for groups of 20+ during the week, so you can't go there.)

Centre Belge de la Bande Dessinée, because it's devoted to cartoons and comic strips, particularly the work of Hergé.

2 life's a beach club, page 74
a) Paradis has windsurfing, surfing, diving and pedalos; La Nivelle has general watersports and canoe hire; La Rhune has no watersports on offer, but you can hire boats; Ravel has sailing and windsurfing.
b) La Nivelle and La Rhune have gym and bike hire.
c) Club la Nivelle.
d) You can also go swimming hire a canoe, go horse-riding and play pelote.

unit 7

1 which wine? page 78
The Muscadet.

a) Muscadet b) Fitou c) Crémant de Loire.

2 just desserts, page 80
peaches (250g), cherries (150g), apples (250g), a lemon

Possible phrases you might need:
Bonjour! Je voudrais deux cents cinquante grammes de pêches. S'il vous plait, donnez-moi cent cinquante grammes de cerises. Je voudrais (aussi) deux cents cinquante grammes de pommes et un citron. Ça fait combien? C'est combien? Voilà.

3 money matters, page 82
When you buy two packets of cheese you get a reduction of 50 cents at the checkout; when you buy two bottles you get the second one half price.

You can't use travellers' cheques – you'll have to use your Visa card.

unit 8

1 shopping heaven, page 86
4th first, then ground floor for the parfumerie, 3rd for the toy and 5th for the CD and computer game.

2 it's a gift! page 88
a) Everything except the scarf and T-shirt. b) Yes, but it costs 1€ per item. c) Credit card but not Diners Card, only American Express.
d) Yes, if you spend more than 100€ and if your hotel is in the first arrondissement. e) You get two hours' free parking if you spend more than 30€.

3 dream jeans, page 90
a) S'il vous plaît, je voudrais un jean noir. b) Je fais du quarante quatre.
c) Je peux l'essayer? d. Ça coûte combien? e. Oui, ça va, je le prends.

4 teething troubles, page 93
a) One tablet every four hours,

preferably with meals, swallow with a large glass of water. b) 6 tablets or 1200mg. c) Yes, you can. d) The tablets are suitable for headaches but she can't have one, because you're warned that if you have asthma you shouldn't take them.

unit 9

1 footballers' lives, page 96
He enjoys the cinema, relaxing, shopping and cooking.

a) l'attaquant vedette.
b) le meilleur club de football de France. c) J'aime bien me promener. d) Je vis tout seul.
e) un peu de tout. f) J'aime tout!

2 social butterfly, page 98
You can't accept Chantal's invitation because you won't be back until 7pm, and you can't accept Robert's invitation as he only has two tickets to the concert, and there are three of you. However, you can accept Florence's invitation to go to the jazz bar with her and her friends.

3 so stylish, page 100
Personal choice!

unit 10

1 match made in heaven? page 104
Personal choice!

2 where in the world? page 106
a) le rosbif – roast beef; la paëlla – paella; le haggis – haggis; le fromage emmenthal – Emmenthal cheese;

les hamburgers – hamburgers; le vodka – vodka.
b) la Tamise – the Thames; la plage de Bondi – Bondi beach; la Statue de la Liberté – the Statue of Liberty; le Kremlin – the Kremlin.
c) une course de taureaux – bull fight; danser le flamenco – dance the flamenco; porter un kilt – wear a kilt; faire de l'escalade – to rock climb; faire du ski – go skiing; un match de base-ball – a baseball game.

Answers to quiz:
1. Espagne 2. Écosse 3. Australie
4. Suisse 5. États-Unis 6. Russie

3 daylight robbery, page 109
You haven't yet written a list of what was stolen, giving the value of each item.

4 get packing! page 110
Sunglasses, swimming costume, walking shoes and sun cream if you want to go walking, but no waterproofs or warm clothes are likely to be needed.

5 postcard from Paris, page 112
Salut!
Ça va? On passe *dix* jours à Paris. Il fait beau, mais hier il a *fait gris*. On a visité *le Louvre* et *Montmartre* et on est montés à la tour Eiffel. Demain on va visiter le Musée *Picasso*.
Bien amicalement.

keep talking french!

If you would like to continue to improve your French, BBC Languages has an extensive selection of other course books and resources. *The French Experience* will take you to the next level of fluency using a combination of print, audio, TV and online. For more information visit www.bbclanguages.com or, to order a catalogue, call 020 8433 3135.

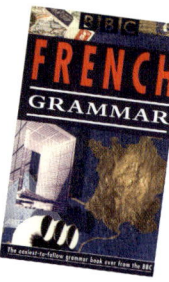

French Grammar
Handy and authoritative reference guide

Independent study course
224pp course book; 5 audio CDs or 4 × 90-minute audio cassettes; 10-part TV series; free online activities

Independent study course
288pp course book; 4 audio CDs or 4 × 75-minute audio cassettes; 20-part TV series; free online activities

don't stop now!

You can add another language to your repertoire with *Get Into Spanish*. With all of the same easy-to-use features, interactive activities and information, you'll be speaking the language in no time! Your journey begins in a typical Spanish town where you can explore all of the same range of people and places that you got to know so well in France. To order your copy, phone our hotline today on 08705 210292.

You can pick up a wide range of other languages with BBC Languages. Log on to *www.bbclanguages.com*